Orientation Systems of the North Pacific Rim

MONOGRAPHS ON GREENLAND
Vol. 352

MAN & SOCIETY
Vol. 42

Michael Fortescue

Orientation Systems of the North Pacific Rim

MUSEUM TUSCULANUM PRESS
UNIVERSITY OF COPENHAGEN
2011

Orientation Systems of the North Pacific Rim

Layout, composition and cover design: Erling Lynder
Printed in Denmark by Specialtrykkeriet Viborg
ISBN 978 87 635 3568 7

Monographs on Greenland | Meddelelser om Grønland, vol. 352
ISSN 0025 6676

Man & Society, vol. 42
ISSN 0106 1062
Series editor: Hans Christian Gulløv

www.mtp.dk/MoG

Cover photo:
Orientation in the Arctic: a Greenlandic woman points out to sea.
Photo: Arctic Institute, Copenhagen.

This book is published with financial support from
The Carlsberg Foundation
E. Lerager Larsens Fond

Museum Tusculanum Press
Njalsgade 126
DK-2300 Copenhagen S
Denmark
www.mtp.dk

Table of Contents

Acknowledgements

I would like to thank all of the native speakers and scholars without whose help this monograph would have been a much more paltry thing. I simply list them here by language in the chronological order in which they appear. I trust that the invaluable information and comments they have provided me with is not misrepresented in any way – responsibility for failings of this kind is entirely my own.

Matt Davidson (Makah); Adam Werle (Ditidaht); Pewi Alfred, Bill Robertson, Billy Peters, Audrey Wilson, Douglas Scow, Jack Nolie, Spruce Wamiss (Kwak'wala); Emmon Bach, Louisa Smith (Haisla); Margaret Anderson, Doug Brown, Douglas Robertson, Max Harris (Sm'algyax); Marie-Louise Tarpent (Nisga'a); Bruce Digsby (Gitksan); Jeff Leer, John Ritter (Tlingit); Michael Krauss (Eyak); Dena'ina (Jim Kari); Walkie Charles, Steve Jacobson (Central Alaskan Yupik); Igor Krupnik (Chukchi); Megami Kurebito (Koryak); and Johanna Mattissen (Nivkh).

I am grateful to the Carlsberg Foundation for supporting my field work in British Columbia and to Linea Ivalo Lykkehøj Michael for the maps and figures (much more presentable than my original sketches), also to both the Carlsberg Foundation and E. Lerager Larsens Fond for partial support of this publication.

Acknowledgements

1. Introduction

The purpose of this investigation is to plot the orientation systems of all the languages spoken along the North Pacific Rim (the northern half of the "Ring of Fire") between the islands of Sakhalin and Hokkaido on the Asian side and Vancouver Island and the Olympic Peninsula on the American side, plus the Arctic coasts adjacent to Bering Strait. By doing so it should be possible to draw out generalizations of an areal and typological nature from a single large-scale region that shares many geophysical traits but where languages belonging to a number of distinct families (or isolates) are situated. This survey can be compared to my earlier work on Eskimo orientation systems all the way from Chukotka to Greenland (Fortescue 1988). In particular, I shall be looking in the synchronic data for diagnostic evidence of diachronic shifts from one kind of geographical environment to another that have occurred in the past. There are various unanswered questions that have been raised in the literature about early movements of language groups in one direction or another within the region which this data can help elucidate – and some of the findings should also be relevant for other parts of the world.[1]

As a first stage I simply gathered together all the data on directional expressions that could be gleaned from reliable sources for the languages concerned, supplemented by my own field work along the British Columbian coast. I then drew a series of schematic maps for individual areas, abstracting the essential oppositions and axes and adding them to the relevant sections of the overall coastline. Map 1 covers the whole region and indicates the general types of system found (CAY = Central Alaskan Yupik, CSY = Central Siberian Yupik). The language families and isolates involved are (from east to west): Wakashan, Tsimshianic, Haida, Tlingit, Eyak, Athabaskan, Eskimo-Aleut, Chukotko-Kamchatkan, Tungusic, Nivkh and Ainu, with some additional information concerning Salishan and Yukaghir added. This raw morpho-lexical data may fall into more or less neat mini-systems, depending on the language (or family), but I have attempted in all cases to abstract the "core" parameters which speakers of these languages – all traditionally

1. cf. Brown (1983) for an early survey of some of the systems that are found elsewhere.

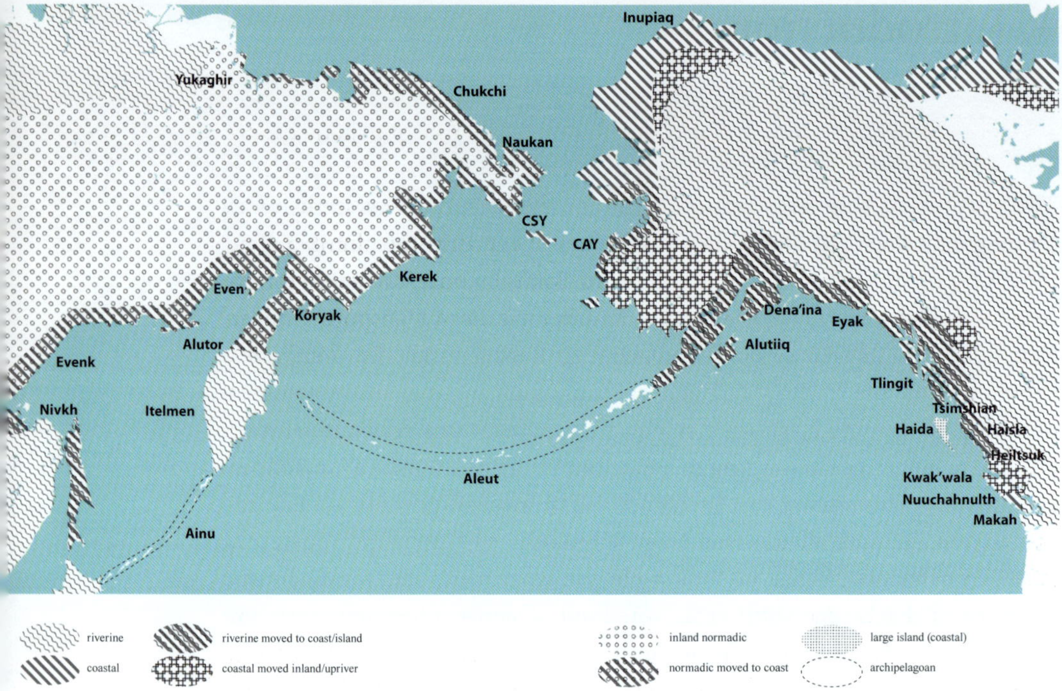

Map 1 Orientation systems of the North Pacific Rim.

hunter-gatherers or fishermen or (Sub-)Arctic nomads – use in order to describe movements and directions in and around their natural habitats. All of the languages concerned are endangered (if not recently extinct) and already many of the original systems are showing signs of overlay by calques from English (or Russian) for the major cardinal directions, most of their speakers being bilingual or monolingual in the majority language and leading sedentary lives today. It is usually apparent when this is happening.

The physical setting of the languages of the North Pacific Rim is very varied, ranging from the temperate rain forests of Vancouver Island through the seasonally ice-blocked coasts of Bering Strait (and adjacent Arctic coasts) and the windswept islands of the Alaskan archipelago, to the almost treeless tundra of Chukotka, the high volcanic mountains of Kamchatka, and the boreal forests of Siberia that reach as far as the Okhotsk coast and Sakhalin. It takes in broad rivers, rich with salmon, glacier-draped mountain ranges, and literally thousands of islands both large and small, some inhabited, many not. A number of different biotic zones are straddled in this huge region, which stretches between latitudes 50 and 70 (and beyond) and between sea level and great mountain peaks reaching many thousands of feet – often straight from the water's edge. Also great extremes in climate are encountered, ranging from the mild, rainy coasts of Vancouver Island to the freezing arctic tundra (and the still colder, but drier interiors of Alaska and Siberia). There is, concomitantly, considerable variation in types of dwelling. In some areas (notably the great rivers and flooded glacial valleys of the British Columbian and adjacent Alaskan coasts) nearly all transportation is by boat, the dense forests and high mountains presenting barriers to other means of transport, while in other areas such as inland Chukotka nomads follow their reindeer herds over vast open territories. In the interior of Alaska there is more varied terrain and flora, and travel (often by dog-sledge) is between or along waterways of varying size hemmed in by massive mountain ranges. Common to the whole region is the proximity of the great ocean and its extension into the Arctic through Bering Strait – all of the peoples concerned in this study either live right on its shores or in the past had regular contact with those that did.

Just as varied are the linguistic means whereby the orientation systems of different languages have adapted to these surroundings, in particular as regards how systematically their orientation systems are morphologically or lexically expressed (see Appendix 1). Whereas all the languages of the North Pacific Rim have rich means of expressing spatial orientation, it is only Na-Dene, Eskimo-Aleut, and Nivkh that (each in their own way) have systems tightly integrated into the grammar as morphological paradigms. In other languages there is a looser collection of "landmark" directionals supplemented by wind terms; some are more variable or local than others and may be ambiguous depending on whether they are applied to local or larger regions. Some languages express directions by means of special "locational" parts of speech, while others apply a sub-set of systems that have a broader application – such as the Eskimo-Aleut demonstrative roots, the Wakashan lexical suffixes, or the Haida proclitics – or else use a combination of such sub-systems. I have summarized the use of morphological means of expressing directions in a separate Appendix 2 since these are so characteristic of the Northwest Coast linguistic area and one might expect some diffusion of the patterns that emerge. In all cases, however, we find a handful of more or less orthogonal axes whose intersection allows speakers to describe location or direction in terms perfectly suited to their given physical environment.

As can be seen from Map 1, there are five main types of orientation system in the languages of the North Pacific Rim and adjacent Arctic coasts:

(a) a purely coastal or maritime one (as in Southern Wakashan and Siberian Yupik)
(b) a purely riverine one (as in inland Central Alaskan Yupik and Itelmen)
(c) an inland nomadic one (as in "reindeer" Chukchi and Even)
(d) an archipelagoan one (as in Aleut)
(e) a "large island" one (as in Haida)

The first is distinguished by "dedicated" up/down coast terms at right angles to a 'down/out-to-sea' vs. 'up/onto-land' axis, all shifting in absolute direction as the coastline shifts its orientation.[2] Such a system has (as described in Fortescue 1988) the possibility of both mirror-image and homologous relationships across bodies of water (depending for example on their size), and often has wind terms varying in absolute direction according to coastal configuration – like its purely directional terms. The second type is geared to a primary 'upriver/downriver' axis (which may be extended to the shores of lakes and bays), with an 'up-from-river' vs. 'down-to-river' dimension applicable to either bank; it does not otherwise display mirror-image extensions. The third type involves neither coast- nor river-specific distinctions (but typically refers to movements of the sun and/or prevailing winds), while the fourth has terms referring uniformly towards and away from one end of an island chain (plus an orthogonal axis that does not shift according to position around individual island coasts). The final type, the "large island" system, is less easily defined except by lack of the traits typifying the others and may be just a variant of (a): in Haida at least it displays a major 'in to coast' vs. 'out to sea' axis that varies in absolute direction around its coast but no dedicated 'up coast' vs. 'down coast' terms.[3]

All five systems, with the possible exception of some varieties of (a), are "absolute" in the sense of Levinson (2003), who distinguishes three main types of "frames of reference", differently utilized across the world's languages. These are the "relative", the "inherent" and the "absolute" frames of reference (all of which may be present in a given language, but weighted

2. There may be distinct 'upriver/downriver' or 'up inlet/down inlet' terms, but these are generally not the same as those used for up and down the coast.
3. In fact (e) may even best be viewed as a variant of (b), since the other major axis in Haida is 'up/down strait/river' and the 'out to sea/onto land' axis applies also locally to these waterways. In that case I would consider the Ainu of Hokkaido also to represent a "large island" system, applicable to both coasts and rivers, although, as will be seen, there is evidence of relatively late adaptation to coastal life in the case of Ainu.

differently in practical application). The first takes the observer's viewpoint as starting point, i.e. in locating an object in front of, behind, or to the left or right of the observer. The inherent frame assigns a natural front, back, top, etc. to an object irrespective of observer viewpoint. And the last of them, the "absolute" frame of reference, positions an object in an objective grid of dimensions applied across a spatial territory irrespective of both the observer's orientation and of the inherent "faces" of objects positioned within the territory. The absolute type is reflected in the cardinal directions of modern European languages and in the dead-reckoning capabilities of speakers of many aboriginal Australian languages, but also embraces a variety of "landmark" systems anchored in a more concrete fashion to the geographical environment of a linguistic community, such as a major river or coastline. It is the latter kind of "absolute" system that this survey will be mostly concerned with, although elements of the "relative" frame of reference ("left" vs. "right") will be touched upon. I shall return to this theoretical framework in the concluding section of the study.

Wind terms – a crucial aspect of the systems I shall be concerned with – may share the same roots as the purely directional terms of the language or be independent of them, but this cuts across my five system types and has more to do with the morpho-lexical resources of the language concerned. Some languages (mainly coastal) do not distinguish clearly between wind names and purely directional terms, but if they have morphological means of doing so they will typically mark the wind terms with some kind of ablative or source marker.

There are also various mixed or "shifted" kinds of system, and these are particularly important diagnostically, since they may reflect a diachronic dimension, e.g. relatively recent movements to or from a coastal setting. Generalizations here may help decide questions posed in the past as to whether, for example, the original Eskimo system was riverine or coastal (cf. Fortescue 1988: 24f.) or whether the Na-Dene waterway system was originally riverine or maritime (cf. Leer 1989: 602). Three sub-types in particular should be noted: (i) riverine systems adapted to coastal settings (as those of Kodiak and, in part, Nunivak islands, which have been projected from the mainland variety of Alaskan Yupik); (ii) coastal systems adapted to inland settings (as in Baker Lake and Anaktuvuk Pass Inuit, so called "caribou" or "mountain" Eskimos respectively); and (iii) inland nomadic systems adapted to a coastal setting (as in maritime Chukchi and Koryak). A further possible type might be the extension of a large island coastal system to the mainland opposite, as exemplified by Alaskan Haida, which moved onto what is essentially the Alaskan mainland (actually a large island – Prince of Wales Island – separated from the mainland by a narrow waterway) a couple of hundred years ago.[4]

All this does not, of course, preclude the possibility of coastal systems having developed from riverine systems that in turn developed from coastal ones (or the reverse) at still earlier times. Successive movements of this kind in the same language family may sometimes result in the seemingly illogical hatchings of adjacent language varieties on Map 1, reflecting a movement inland following upon an earlier movement to the coast (or the reverse). Thus the system of Interior Tlingit, which involves the loss of a clear 'upriver/downriver' axis distinct from cardinal 'north/south', appears to be the result of a movement inland within the last two centuries, but that of coastal Tlingit in turn reflects a much earlier movement down to the coast since its system is homologous (and cognate) with that of inland Athabaskan, but adjusted to the coast. Furthermore, some degree of bidirectional adjustment or harmonization may arise between adjacent systems in situations of close contact, as for example between Siberian Yupik and coastal Chukchi, a case which will be taken up in a separate section.

Given the examples of Nunivak and Kodiak islands within the Eskimo world, it should not surprise us to find what looks like riverine systems existing on islands also elsewhere. The riverine system of Nivkh, for example, was transported more or less *en bloc* to western Sakhalin. Such extensions of riverine systems to the coasts from further inland seems quite common along the Northwest American coast, as in the case of Coast Tsimshian, whose orientation system is homologous to the two inland varieties of the Tsimshianic family, and of Eyak on the southern Alaskan coast, which appears to be just as riverine in origin as the inland Athabaskan languages to which it is related. What is perhaps more surprising is that the Northern Wakashan system as in Kwak'wala should appear at first sight to be riverine, as opposed to the purely coastal one of the southern Wakashans (with its "dedicated" up coast/down coast terms independent of 'upriver/downriver' ones). The way of life of all these people is coastal (although only the southern groups developed ocean whaling), in contrast to the decidedly riverine

4. This is a somewhat different case from that of Northern Wakashan, which I do not treat as a large island system. Although branches of it did move off at some stage from northern Vancouver Island, only a relatively narrow strait separates the latter from the mainland, and it would hardly have been conceived of as an island at all.

(or inland waterway-based) way of life of the Salishan tribes.[5] The similarity between the Northern Wakashan and the Coast Tsimshian systems suggest an areal relationship – there is at all events a northern northwest coast cultural sub-area involving these languages, as well as Tlingit and Haida, that is culturally distinct from the more southerly one relating the Nootkans, Chimakuans and Salishans within a central sub-area of the Northwest coast (cf. Scherzer 1976: 142). To decide whether the Northern Wakashan system developed from something more like the Southern Wakashan system or *vice versa* we need to uncover possible diagnostics of riverine systems moving down to the coast – as opposed to the reverse.

One such diagnostic (for a coastal system moving upriver) is, as suggested above, the presence of 'up coast' vs. 'down coast' terms that are no longer "dedicated" like in purely coastal systems, since they have come to be used *also* for 'upstream' vs. 'downstream'. This would introduce a natural ambiguity (two orthogonal interpretations of the same pair of terms), indicating the shift of coast-oriented dwellings to position along river banks. In the case of a riverine system moving out to a coast, this would result rather in a partial freeing of the originally riverine terms from directions along specific waterways, now treating inlets or bays into which major rivers run as themselves river-like bodies. The simplest instance of the latter is Dena'ina Athabaskan (the only coastal variety of Alaskan Athabaskan), where the common Athabaskan 'upriver' vs. 'downriver' terms have simply been extended to Cook Inlet, which opens out like a broad river towards the southwest. A rather more complex case is found in Pacific Coast Yupik Alutiiq, where not only have the common Central Alaskan Yupik 'downriver/upriver' terms been applied to Cook Inlet, but where a number of key wind terms (like *uŋalaq*) have also been 'swivelled' through 90 degrees. Further complications occur on Kodiak Island, but the essential Alutiiq system is preserved, without any of the mirror-image reversals one finds in the Bering Strait or Arctic coast regions between the mainland and large islands (thus the important wind *uŋalaq* is still from the (south)east).

According to the criteria suggested above, it would seem more likely that the Northern Wakashan system (specifically that of Kwak'wala,) was originally coastally orientated (as in Southern Wakashan), with its 'north/south' (or rather 'northwest/southeast') coastal terms becoming applied

5. The widely accepted term "Coast Salish" is therefore somewhat misleading. The movement east that produced "Inland Salish(an)" was secondary (although still ancient).

to 'downriver/upriver' (perhaps specifically on the Nimpkish river). Later, when Northern Wakashan expanded further north along the highly indented mainland coast as well as further to the southeast (absorbing or displacing Salishan groups), it would have taken the riverine/inlet interpretations of its coastal terms with it. What happens still further north in Haisla, whose speakers live on long inlets far inland, is a reversion to a nearly pure riverine interpretation of the Kwak'wala system, entailing a shift of *n'ala-* (the 'south' direction in Kwak'wala) to 'north'. Haisla, note, is the variety of Northern Wakashan most closely integrated into the northern cultural sub-area mentioned above which includes Tsimshian and Tlingit, each with their own riverine systems. In all this area 'north' is roughly equated with 'upriver/up inlet' (the converse equation of 'south' with 'downriver' is not so consistent, except in Tlingit).[6]

Paradoxically, there appear to be traces of the same development in Inuit Eskimo, in so far as the 'inside' demonstrative direction (naturally used for 'upriver' along the Kobuk River, for instance) is specifically applied to 'right-along-the-coast' in northern Alaska, the direction in which the distance between the shore and the permanent sea ice gets smaller, and travel in general gets tougher, against prevailing cold winds. However, this may be coincidental – compare the application of an 'inside' demonstrative to the direction of the Alaskan mainland in archipelagoan Aleut (where there are no rivers at all). It should be borne in mind that the expansion eastward of the almost purely coastal Thule culture of northern Alaska was a much more recent event (some thousand years ago) than the coastal adaptation of the Wakashans (who have lived on the western coast of Vancouver Island for at least 5000 years). I shall return to both the Inuit and the Wakashan cases in following sections.

Any argument for an original riverine as opposed to coastal origin of existing systems must take into consideration the orientation of the traditional dwelling *vis-à-vis* the coast or river bank in the communities concerned, i.e. the relationship between the internal "microcosm" and the external "macrocosm" (as Bergsland put it for Aleut and Krejnovič for Nivkh). The only languages in the region not to display an overlap between terms referring to

6. The 'downriver' and 'upriver' terms of Tsimshian are primary (and etymologically opaque) and their extension to cardinal 'north' and 'south' is only partial. The equation of 'upriver' with (cardinal) 'north' is actually only unambiguous inland, whereas in Coast Tsimshian there is some confusion, which may be the result of contact with English speakers if not areal influence from Tlingit and Northern Wakashan.

directions within the house and those without are the Southern Wakashan and Tsimshianic ones.[7] As an initial hypothesis, I shall suggest that terms for directions within and around the house that are orthogonal to the directions based on the same terms applied along a waterway or shore are indicative of a coastal system that has moved to a riverine setting or *vice versa* (note that houses typically face waterways in both coastal and riverine systems). The direction of the innermost (rear) wall of the house in a "pure" (i.e. original) coastal system, for example, is logically orthogonal to the coastline and points "upland" towards the interior of the land, with no conflict between "microcosmic" and "macrocosmic" uses if the same term is used for both these directions, but if such a system were transferred inland up a river the 'towards rear wall' direction would only locally be 'upland' (up from the river bank), whereas the direction into the interior of the land, away from the coast, would now be 'upriver' (orthogonal to 'upland' and 'towards the rear wall'). If the original 'upland' term remains fixed to its broader 'inland' sense, one can easily see how ambiguity might arise.

A coastal system moving upstream might well continue to apply its 'out-to-sea' vs. 'up-into-land' macrocosmic opposition to the front vs. the rear of dwellings, at least as long as regular contact with the coast is maintained. If such a system moreover applies its 'up coast' vs. 'down coast' opposition to 'upriver' vs. 'downriver' but continues to use it within the house in its original ("absolute") orientation, this would be orthogonal to the flow of the river in the new riverine setting, so the terms used (if still the same) would be ambivalent. This situation is indeed what one finds in inlet-based Northern Wakashan, where the 'up-into-land' vs. 'out-to-sea' terms are used for directions within the house independent of the actual location of the house (always towards/away from the water, whether on the coast or on the bank of a river or inlet), but the 'upriver' vs. 'downriver' ones, referring also to up and down the sea coast, are ambivalent and, it would seem, more transient in their usage within the house, since it is now the macrocosmic 'downriver' vs. 'upriver' dimension that is dominant.

In a "pure" riverine system, such as the watershed-based Athabaskan one, there is a natural correlation of the directions 'towards the rear of the house' with 'upland' (away from the river) and 'towards the front of the house' with 'downland', i.e. with slope rather than water flow being criterial. If a

7. These all have a welter of spatial suffixes or proclitics with specific meanings. Also Itelmen on the Asian side seems to lack this connection (though the data is limited).

riverine system is brought down permanently to the coast, the new orientation of the house towards the ocean will logically result in ambivalence (at least initially): the 'downland' vs. 'upland' opposition will naturally align with 'seaward' vs. 'landward' (and will still have an unchanged natural application within the house), but the 'upriver' vs. 'downriver' terms (parallel with the front of the house) will now align both with 'up coast' vs. 'down coast' and with the original riverine directions along the river down which the system was brought. The latter usage (maintaining the same "absolute" orientation *vis-à-vis* the river) could well determine how the front and back walls of the house on the coast continue to be designated. This could be long-lasting, blocking the more logical use of the 'seaward' vs. 'landward' terms for this purpose, since the "macrocosmic" use of the latter pair is now dominant.

The fact that the Athabaskan system consistently – and unambiguously – distinguishes the 'uphill / downhill' dimension from the 'upriver / downriver' one within the house as well as outside it suggests a very old and stable inland system, one that was not linked to a particular waterway, but applicable to any watershed system (a distinct advantage amongst people constantly traveling around over vast interior tracts).[8] Central Alaskan Yupik is interesting, since it seems only partially to reflect a purely riverine system: here 'towards the rear of the house' is expressed by the 'inside' demonstrative, which is also used for 'upriver', whereas 'towards the front of the house' is simply 'down'. This suggests an ancient adaptation to riverine location, but one in which there are still traces of the system's origins on the coast.

In what follows I shall look at the individual sub-regions of the North Pacific Rim one by one (according to language family), in order to show how their orientation systems are organized, both as regards the geographical setting, the interior of the house, and (where this is a separate issue) the relationship between the two. *En route* I shall investigate the possible source of the unusual conflation between house-internal 'towards the fire' and a house-external 'out onto the water' terms (and their converse, 'away from the fire' and 'to the shore') displayed by a number of the languages concerned. In many of the languages of the survey it will be seen that the same terms may be used on more than one "scale", typically the immediate area

8. As Kari points out (pers. comm.), the individual area to which such a system applies is the watershed of a single major river – rather than being repeated at different angles up every minor tributary or following language / dialect boundaries exactly.

surrounding the house or village on the one hand as opposed to the wider region (e.g. a language or dialect area) on the other. The local usage will generally be more flexible (dependent on local configurations of the landscape). The directions in the wider, areal usage will generally be more stable or fixed. I shall attempt finally to derive some generalizations concerning idiosyncracies that can be diagnostic for moves from one geographical setting to another in pre-historic times. It will be seen in particular whether the "orthogonality hypothesis" sketched above can hold up or will need modifying.

2. The Wakashan family: coast vs. inlet

The orientation systems of the Wakashan languages range from purely coastal in the south (Makah, Ditidaht and Nuuchahnulth – previously "Nootka") to almost purely riverine in the far north (Haisla), with an interesting transitional area in the middle (Kwak'wala and Oowekyala/Heiltsuk). This reflects the prehistoric movements of the Northern Wakashan people southeastward up Queen Charlotte Strait from their probable homeland around the northern tip of Vancouver Island, whence there must once have been a continuum of coastal tribes down into Southern Wakashan territory, and then northward across the strait and up the highly indented mainland coast. The areal or substratum influence exerted by Salishan or Tsimshianic groups in this process is uncertain, though it is known that the expansion did absorb or displace a number of Salishan groups.[9]

The southern, coastal system – which I would suggest lies closest to the Proto-Wakashan system – is typified by dedicated 'up coast' vs. 'down coast' terms, although the first term of the pair is unfortunately not attested for Ditidaht or recently extinct Makah. Davidson (pers. comm.) indicates that Makah used either one of its 'out to sea' terms or the stem meaning 'return home' for 'down strait', and this may well have been true of Ditidaht too. Nuuchahnulth has respectively suffix *-inˀatu* and *hitaqtliƚ* (with "empty" stem *hit-* plus suffixes *-aqtl* 'inside' and *-iƚ* 'in the house').[10] The Nuuchahnulth is for the Tsishaath dialect, recorded in great detail by Sapir – this was originally spoken on the islands in Barkley Sound although today its speakers are to be found far up the inlet at Port Alberni, where they were moved in the 1920s,

9. There was a much later expansion of Kwak'wala speakers down Johnstone Strait further to the southeast at the expense of the Salishan Comox, but this resulted only in the formation of an easternmost dialect of Kwak'wala (Lekwiltok), not in the appearance of new languages, as with Oowekyala and Heiltsuk to the north.

10. *-in¿atu* (with pharyngeal /¿/ as opposed to glottal /?/) is perhaps related to Proto-Wakashan *-a(:)X* 'down' and *-a:t(u:)* 'down(stream)' (thus Makah *-aq'atu* and Nuuchahnulth *-¿a:ʔat,* Ditidaht *-¿a:ʔt* 'move down') – the nasal in Nuuchahnulth could reflect *-n'i* ~ *-in-* 'arrive at'. If so, the opposition between a 'down' and an 'in' term for up and down the coast has a remarkable – but probably coincidental – parallel in the coastal Eskimo world. *-aqtliƚ* can be contrasted with *-aqtl'as* 'in the woods, interior' with *-as* 'on the ground'.

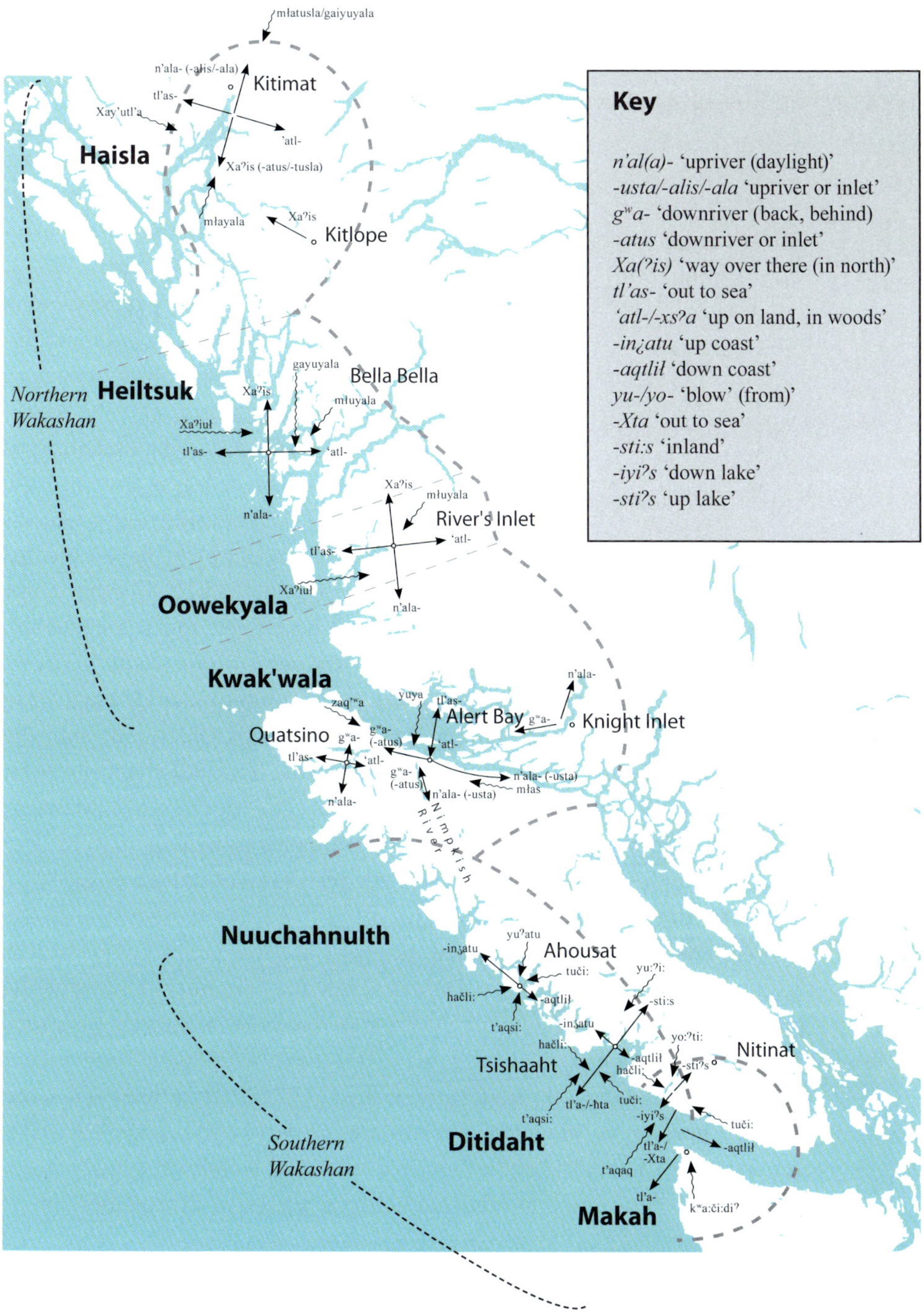

Map 2 Wakashan.

just as Ditidaht speakers were moved inland to the village of Nitinat at the far end of the lake of that name. I have indicated the directionals for both languages on Map 2 near the coast since the systems in both of them are clearly still coastal in nature. Note that winds, as opposed to pure directionals, are indicated by wiggly lines, as on all the maps. There is reliable data for two other Nuuchahnulth dialects besides Tsishaath in the south, namely Ahousaht (also shown on the map) and Kyuquot further to the north (virtually identical to the other two as regards directionals).

It should be pointed out that Makah and Ditidaht are very close to each other (forming a "Straits" sub-group of Southern Wakashan) and that Ditidaht may in fact represent the result of a blend of Makah, brought back to Vancouver Island by a break-away group returning north, and the southernmost variety of Nuuchahnulth (cf. Fortescue 2007: 1). The Makah wind directions shared with Ditidaht are orientated more or less in the same absolute directions as there, not in a mirror image relationship, e.g. *k'ʷa:či:diʔ* 'south wind' and *yu:ʔati* (Ditidaht *yo:ʔti*) 'north wind' (which I have indicated each only once for both languages on the map, due to lack of space – also east wind *tuči:* and west wind *haha:čƛi* could have been added for Makah). The same is true of the direction of the 'down coast' suffix *-aqtlił* (here better glossed as 'up sound (to east)'), which points up into Juan de Fuca Strait in both languages. Only the Ditidaht directional suffix *-a(d'a)* 'out onto the water' is the opposite of corresponding Makah *-a-*, but these naturally point out to sea in any direction that the sea lies. Also *tl'a:-* 'out to sea' in Makah is apparently homologous with the direction referred to by that stem in Ditidaht (namely out to the ocean to the southwest) rather than across the strait to Vancouver Island parallel with suffix *-a-*.[11]

There are 'up/downriver or inlet' terms in all these languages (as well as distinct 'up/down lake' ones in Ditidaht), but they are not the same as the 'up coast/down coast' ones. All are expressed almost exclusively by lexical suffixes (added to stems/lexical roots of motion), with "path" (movement to or from) and location often distinguished by separate suffixes. Thus the Ditidaht 'upriver' vs. 'downriver' terms are, respectively, *-a:d'awt*l (or *-a:d'ƛ*) and *-Xsuw*; the former is etymologically 'all along length of' (plus 'place'), and the latter (not found in Nuuchahnulth) is related to Proto-Nootkan *-Xt*

11. The accuracy of this item (i.e. *tl'a:ʔas* 'south') from Davidson (2002) is not entirely certain however (Davidson pers. comm.). Note that the Makah themselves were referred to in Nuuchahnulth and Ditidaht as *tl'a:ʔasʔatḥ* 'people out to sea' (at Neah Bay).

'downstream, out of the woods' and/or Proto-Wakashan *-(k)sawi* 'through' (cf. Kwak'wala *-(x)siu* 'mouth of river').[12] 'Downstream' and 'out of the woods (downland)' are also conflated in the Nuuchahnulth suffix *-a:t*. The orthogonal 'inland/out to sea' axis is expressed by the opposing suffixes *-sti:s* vs. *-Xta/-ħta,* (the last of these paired with lexical root *tl'a:-* as in *tl'a:ʔas* 'seaward' and *tl'eeʔił* 'seaward side, sound'). These are found all along the west coast of Vancouver Island as far as the abrupt border with Quatsino Kwak'wala in the north, as are the principal wind terms (expressed by more or less opaque lexical stems). There are a great many combinations of spatial lexical suffixes with "empty" stems (*hit-, hił-* and *hin-/hid-*), as also in Northern Wakashan. Thus, for example, Nuuchahnulth *hina:čitl* 'go out to sea', *hiłwaħsuł* 'mouth of a river', *hitasatl* 'come to land', *hinusčis* 'up the beach', *hitaħt'a* 'move downstream, through rapids', and *hitaqu:ʔa* 'come round a point'.

This system (though not its expression) is reminiscent of the coastal Inuit one – though without the residual microcosmic/macrocosmic "ambiguity" found there and without as much local variation, understandably since the west coast of Vancouver Island lies along a general northwest/southeast axis. The common "skeleton" of the system consists of the 'in to the shore' vs. 'out to sea' suffixes and the 'up/down coast' ones completed by suffixes meaning 'down to the shore/beach' vs. 'up from the shore/beach' (Nuuchahnulth *-n'iqis* vs. *-w'isč* (Ditidaht *-ad'iʔs* vs. *-wišč*). There are no "odd" applications of macrocosmic directionals within the house or vice versa, though of course there are words (or rather suffixes) referring to the rear vs. the front of the house and its walls. A further parallel to coastal Inuit system is suggested by Nuuchahnulth *čim-ciiy'as* (lit. 'right-at end/edge') exemplified by Stonham (2005) with reference to the 'righthand' side of a village, this being determined by the perspective of someone looking out to sea. This picture is not surprising for a specialized maritime culture that has been in place in the region for several millennia, with dwellings consistently fronting the ocean.

The situation in Northern Wakashan is more complicated. There are surprisingly few cognate terms shared by the orientation systems of the two rather distantly related branches of the family. A notable exception is the

12. The Ditidaht 'up lake' term *-stiʔs* corresponds to Nuuchahnulth *-sti:s* 'up inlet' (Kyuquot dialect) or 'move into interior' (Tsishaath dialect). The opposite, *-iyiʔs,* corresponds to Nuuchahnulth *-wi:ʔis* 'go down to the coast' (Tsishaath). Thanks to Adam Werle for these. These are compound suffixes combining more basic ones (e.g. *-wi* 'go out' and *-is* 'on the beach' in the latter case).

'out to sea' stem *tl'a:-/tl'as-*, and the corresponding suffix (Nuuchahnulth *-ħta*, Kwak'wala *-(X)t'a)* – a suitable reminder of the common maritime origins of the whole family.[13] The system in Kwak'wala was well described by Boas (1909 and 1934), but his information was limited to the central "Kwakiutl" dialect area on the northeast coast of Vancouver Island around Fort Rupert. In my own fieldwork I have attempted to elicit a more detailed coverage of how the same basic system applies to different localities within this geographically complex area. This broader picture can also shed some light on the diachronic development of the system. The evidence seems to point in the direction of an early riverine system in the Kwak'wala area, at least for the northeast coast of Vancouver Island, one focused on the salmon-rich Nimpkish valley (lake and river), which was perhaps initially utilized only during seasonal activities. This probably developed out of an earlier "Proto-Wakashan" coastal system when speakers of Northern Wakashans first moved into the inner waterways of northeastern Vancouver Island (I return to this below in connection with the system at Quatsino). The many inlets in the region would not have been conceptualized differently from rivers like the Nimpkish as regards orientation up and down them.

One further step in very recent times can be seen as the result of the forced concentration during the last century of the Nimpkish Kwakwak'awakw (and speakers from other adjacent dialect areas) on the small island of Alert Bay, where an infamous "residential" school was situated. This is an example of a riverine system being transplanted to an island setting, one which until then had only been used seasonally. The situation around the Nimpkish River estuary is schematized in Figure 1, where the position of the house on the coast and the river respectively is indicated with some "microcosmic" directions added (these are divided between the two house schemas due to lack of space); for *GəmX-* and *hił-* see below, otherwise the figure shares the same key as that to Map 1.[14]

How is it possible that the "original" Kwak'wala system could have been riverine if the Proto-Wakashan one was not? The situation here is in fact

13. Note also *yuya*, the cold north(east) wind in Kingcome Inlet and elsewhere in Kwak'wala (literally blowing out of an inlet), which has near cognates in Southern Wakashan, e.g. *yu:ʔi:* the north wind in Nuuchahnulth (based on the Proto-Wakashan root *yu(:)-* 'blow (wind)').

14. Note the suffixes for 'up the beach' (*-usdis*), 'down the beach' (*-nc'is*), 'down to the shore' (*-wułta*), 'in to the shore' (*-idłis(la)*, 'up from the shore' (*-y'ag*) and 'out from the shore' (*-we'*).

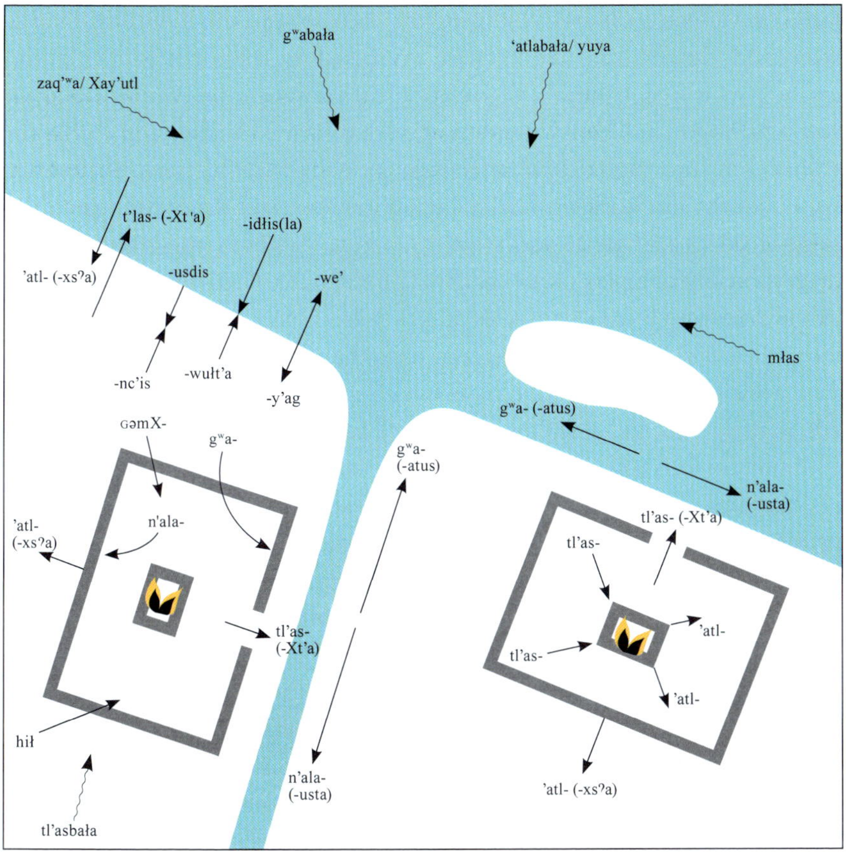

Fig. 1 Kwak'wala directions (schematic).

quite different from in "true" riverine systems of the Salishan kind.[15] The essential point to bear in mind as regards Kwak'wala is that 'upriver' and 'up strait' (i.e. up Queen Charlotte Strait towards narrower Johnstone Strait) are expressed by the same term, namely *n'ala-* (also meaning 'daylight'), which is generally interpreted as 'south' – precisely the direction the Nimpkish flows

15. The typical Salishan system is, much like the Athabaskan one, based on a simple crossing of two axes, '(downland) towards river, out from shore' (e.g. Upper Halkomelem *ta·l* or *cucu*) vs. 'away from the river, (up) towards backwoods' (U.H. *ca·ləq^{w}*), and 'upriver' (U.H. *tiył*) vs. 'downriver' (U.H. *ła·s*). Winds based on these and similar terms point in the direction expected from the orientation of the river or inlet concerned. Kuipers (2002) reconstructs the following Proto-Salishan stems: **kaw* 'down (e.g. to river bank or beach)'; **k^{w}um* 'up, ashore, inland', **tl'aX* 'upstream', and **yəx^{w}/ləx^{w}* 'down (stream)'.

from on Vancouver Island, emerging at the coast opposite Alert Bay. 'Downriver' and 'down strait' are likewise expressed by the same root, *gʷa-* (literally 'backwards, behind'), the relationship between the two senses again being orthogonal. The corresponding verbal forms *n'alułəla* and *gʷołəla* (or *gʷolisəla*) for moving in these directions are equally ambivalent. So, confusingly, 'south' and 'east' (in cardinal geographic terms) are expressed by the same word, as are 'north' and 'west'.[16] Context – and to some extent varying derivational extensions – will usually disambiguate. Crossing the *n'ala-/gʷa-* axis everywhere is the opposition of *'atl-* 'inland, behind the village, into the woods' vs. *tl'as-* 'towards the sea, out onto the water (sea, river or inlet)'. All four principal directions have corresponding lexical suffixes (quite unrelated), namely *-usta* vs. *-atus* ('up' and 'down' respectively) and *-xsʔa* ('from sea to shore, up into woods') vs. *-Xt'a* ('out to sea'). This basic picture holds for all local varieties of Kwak'wala. The potential ambiguity becomes extreme at sites like Kingcome Inlet, which is set inside a deep inlet on the northern side of Queen Charlotte Strait, opposite from Alert Bay: here *n'ala-* is (locally) 'up inlet' (to the north), but in a broader areal sense still 'south', a sense shared by all Kwak'wala speakers to refer to the direction of Vancouver – actually to the southeast. Similarly, *gʷabała*, the southerly wind blowing upriver at Kingcome Inlet, is a northerly wind at Alert Bay (blowing up the Nimpkish valley). The situation is very similar in Knight Inlet, further east, where I have marked the upriver/downriver directions.

The situation sketched above shows that these terms may have more than one sense at any given locality, a local (e.g. strictly riverine) vs. a broader regional one. It appears that a quasi-cardinal system (probably glossed on the corresponding English terms) has been superimposed upon an originally local system geared to specific rivers or inlets (we shall see something similar in Coast Tsimshian). This is reminiscent of the way that an absolute cardinal system has been superimposed on the local system of West Greenland as described in Fortescue (1988). However, with Kwak'wala this is not a

16. Actually the whole coast is tilted NW/SE, so we are not talking exactly north, south, etc., here. English glosses of this nature (especially in dictionaries) may be misleading. Thus *gʷolisəla* is used of traveling north(east) to Smith Sound from Alert Bay, and *n'alułəla* of traveling from there (south)east to Cape Mudge (near Campbell River). Another word sometimes glossed as 'west', *qʷiqʷeXseXsulis* ('over the mountains' in Grubb 1977) is built on stem *qʷis-* 'on far side', specifically referring to the west coast of Vancouver Island from a Queen Charlotte Strait point of view (the Southern Wakashans are called *qʷiqʷesaʔzi* there).

straightforward case of direct calques of the English terms – it is still difficult for most speakers to translate 'east' and 'west' with native terms at all. The 'upriver' term *n'ala-* (in derivative form *n'əlziʔ* or *n'əlzikʷ*)[17] is simply used to refer to vague geographical 'south' (explained as 'the direction towards Vancouver'), and *gʷa-* (*gʷaziʔ* or *gʷenakʷ*) is similarly used of vague geographical 'north'. Some speakers go further, however, using not only these terms to gloss the corresponding English terms but also *'atl'i* (lit. 'into the forest, inland') to gloss English 'east' and *tl'asa* ('out onto the water') to gloss 'west'.

There are also wind terms that vary in absolute direction according to location, some of them derived from the four principal directional terms above, others more opaque. The former kind (as illustrated by *gʷabała* above) are highly local, whereas the latter tend to be more stable across the region, for example *młas* is generally a southeast wind and *zaq'ʷa* a northwest one (up and down the east coast of the main island). Other important directional elements include stems *Gʷas-* 'near side' and *qʷis-* 'far side', *ʔəps-* 'on other side', and suffix *-k'ut* 'opposite side', which may combine with other directional stems we have seen, e.g. *gʷak'ut* 'opposite side downriver'. There are numerous possible combinations of stems plus suffixes of this kind – for their widespread application in place names see Boas (1934).[18]

As an example of a sub-region with quite a different geographical disposition from the northeast coast of the main island, consider the following information I received concerning Quatsino (a deep fjord area with its entrance on the Pacific coast – i.e. located in the interior of northwest Vancouver Island). This area has its own dialect, but the directional terms are the same as elsewhere – only applied in a locally divergent way. Thus *tl'as-* is '(west-south-)west' (out to sea through the main inlet, as in *tl'asaʔaqa* 'go out to sea through Quatsino Sound), and *'atl'i* is '(east-north-)east' (up into the interior forest), as expected. However, *gʷa-* and *n'ala-* are more confusing since the local senses ('down/up inlet') are at loggerheads with the wider geographical senses ('north/south'), much as at Kingcome Inlet on the far side of Queen Charlotte Strait. My impression (from talking with just one former resident

17. The distinction in Grubb's dictionary between *n'əldzi* or *neldzixʷ* 'south' and *naldzik* 'east' is spurious.

18. Note also the stems for 'left side' and 'right side' (not limited in Wakashan to the human body as in most languages of the region), thus Kwak'wala *GəmXaniGʷił* 'lefthand side of house – seen from inside house looking out' (with stem *qəmX* 'left'), Haisla *hiłk'udis* 'righthand side of bay, beach, river' (from *hił-* 'right' plus *-k'ut* 'side' plus *-is* 'on beach'), also Nuuchahnulth *čimcaqs* '(at) righthand side of vessel'.

of Quatsino village) is that the "broader" sense of these terms tends to prevail in most situations – also in describing the different walls of the house, i.e. the north ("downriver") vs. the south ("upriver") wall respectively. Obviously this is at odds with the local senses of the 'up/downriver' (i.e. 'up/down inlet') terms around Quatsino Sound, but it is consistent with the notion that the system at Quatsino has come inland up the sound from its original coastal position. The opposing terms *gʷa-* and *n'ala-* are still used in their local senses for going up or down either of the long side inlets of the inside end of the main sound. To go up and down the main channel itself the forms *laʔeglis(əla)* 'go up inlet' vs. *law'e(la)* 'go down inlet' are used, as also at Kingcome Inlet.

As regards the orientation of the house in Kwak'wala generally, the situation described by Boas (1909) for the northeast coast of the island, whereby the outside of the house facing the water was known as *tl'asanuʔi* (from *tl'as-* 'seaward' and *-nuʔi* 'side') as opposed to *'atl'anuʔi* (from *'atl-* 'inland'), still pertains, irrespective of the actual cardinal direction in which the house faces (most but not all houses still face the water). The corresponding internal sides of the house, *gʷanuʔi* for the 'downriver' side and *n'alanuʔi* for the 'upriver' side, could only be confirmed by some of my older consultants however.[19] It should not be forgotten that the old style house with the central fireplace is now a thing of the past. Some speakers do not distinguish between inside or outside walls, as was the case at Quatsino. Here, as described above, the opposition is natural in so far as *n'ala-* 'south' (used for the south wall) matches its etymological source, 'daylight', and *gʷa-* 'north' (used for the north wall) is indeed "behind" the northwest end of the island, as the etymology suggests. This may reflect the original coastal sense of all these terms, before the movement of Kwak'wala-speaking groups to the east side of the island (and further north from there). The rather unintuitive swiveling by 90 degrees of the *gʷa-/n'ala-* axis on the northeast coast as applied to within the house (bringing it in line with the *tl'as-/'atl-* axis) would

19. This riverine usage may be secondary, the result of Kwak'wala speakers moving up the Nimpkish river while maintaining the actual coastal senses of the two terms. If the houses were still oriented with their fronts towards the water there would have been conflict between the application of the terms to the interior of the house and to the river itself. There would not have been such ambiguity with the 'seaward' vs. 'landward' terms (the most important axis, since the 'seaward' wall is the ones containing the doorway between the microcosm and the macrocosm). 'Landward' can of course be understood as 'up from the river bank', and 'seaward' as 'down to the river bank' (on either side of a river).

have come later, part of the same adjustment to riverine/inlet use of the system in the area that Boas investigated.[20] The 'seaward' vs. 'landward' opposition referring to house walls evidently transported better as microcosmic, house-internal directions than the 'upriver' vs. 'downriver' opposition (with its inherent ambiguity), and ended up reaching as far up the coast as Haisla, where the Wakashan family borders with Tsimshianic. See the section on Fire and Water for the further use in all the Northern Wakashan languages of the 'out to sea' vs. 'inland' terms to refer to movement towards or away from the central fireplace in the traditional house.

Let me pursue this question of distinguishing the case of a riverine system becoming coastal from the reverse a little further. It is reasonable to assume that it is indeed a matter of the reverse in the case of the shift from the original northwest Vancouver Island coast system – if my analysis of it is correct – to both the Quatsino system today and the Nimpkish one. But what of the Kwak'wala system as applied at Alert Bay, where the population from the Nimpkish river valley have been concentrated on an island totally lacking in rivers? It certainly looks like a case of a riverine system projected to the coast – and to the islands off it. As expected, the original 'up/downriver' terms are still consistently applied to up and down Queen Charlotte Strait, as well as to the north/south axis up and down the Nimpkish valley. The etymology of the 'south' term, *n'ala-* ('daylight') would support the likelihood of the Nimpkish valley north/south axis simply being extended out into the sound to the island in this fashion – it is unlikely at least that the influence was from the northern side of the strait, where 'upriver' is to the north.

To be more specific about the original Proto-Northern Wakashan system, it is reasonable to suppose that on the west coast near the mouth of Quatsino Sound (home of the Tl'ask'inuxw tribe, literally 'the seaward people', southernmost of the Quatsino groups) there was an original coastal system similar to that of Southern Wakashan further down the coast. It could have first become applied to a mixed riverine/inlet-based location when the an-

20. This also applies to the suffixes corresponding to movement towards the front or back walls of the house. Farther north, note, in Heiltsuk and Haisla, the *'atlanuʔi/tl'asanuʔi* parts of the house refer to the outside walls, aligning as expected with the macrocosmic direction of the ocean as opposed to inland. (*g*^{w}*a-* and *n'ala-* are not used this way). Compare the "natural" naming of all four walls of the house in the purely riverine Salishan languages. Kuipers (1969), for example, contrasts literal terms for the Squamish 'upriver', 'downriver', 'landward', and 'shoreward' sides of the house (with separate derivations according to whether the longer walls are the landward/shoreward ones or the upriver/downriver ones).

cestors of the Kwak'wala-speaking tribes moved into more peaceable inland waters away from the harsher conditions of the west coast, both up Quatsino Sound and around the north end of the island into Queen Charlotte Strait.[21] The latter too could have been conceived of as a large river with two opposing banks, narrowing towards Johnstone Strait. The system as such would have been taken up the salmon-rich Nimpkish valley at some stage, where it became solidly riverine, but with "orthogonal" traces of its earlier coastal application.

When one looks further north towards the other Northern Wakashan languages, Oowekyala at Rivers Inlet, Heiltsuk at Bella Bella and Haisla at Kitimat and Kitlope, we see a stepwise adjustment of the system (by now more consistently riverine in application) to the deeply indented coastline of the mainland. This reflects the movement north of Wakashan tribes, absorbing or pushing back Salishan and perhaps other groups already in the area. The system of Oowekyala, intermediate in position between Kwak'wala and Heiltsuk, is virtually identical with the latter, so I shall not mention it again.[22] The essential difference between the systems of Heiltsuk and Kwak'wala is formal: the 'north/downstream' term *g*^{w}*a-* is here replaced by another stem *Xa(ʔis),* which is derived from the proto-Wakashan root *Xa-* meaning '(far) over there' and *-'is* 'on the beach'. It is also found in Kwak'wala in the name of a westerly wind (an alternative to *zaq'*^{w}*a*), namely *Xay'utl* (probably with *-itl* 'into house or inlet'). The ambivalence of the 'up/downriver' terms of Kwak'wala manifests itself here in the similarly ambivalent senses of *Xa(ʔis)* and *n'ala-*. This axis lies roughly north/south along the coast (thus with *n'ala-* still pointing south) but (south)east/(north)west up adjacent inlets. The presumably unambiguous senses of *tl'as-* and *'atl-*, forming the orthogonal coastal axis, are maintained with the same orientation as further south, pointing out to sea (west) and inland (east) respectively. Numerous specific

21. About 2,500 years ago, to judge from the archaeological record (cf. Mitchell 1990: 357).

22. I should, however, mention Salishan Bella Coola, spoken inland up a long inlet from the vicinity of Bella Bella, since it has been strongly influenced by Northern Wakashan, both lexically and grammatically. The orientation system remains clearly riverine, of the Salishan kind, with 'downriver' vs. 'upriver' (*taqw'lh* vs. *ʔaaxlh*) being central. Thus the southeast wind *txats'aaxlh*, literally comes from upriver. Nater also has *tx-aqw'lh* 'people from the north, Port Simpson (on the coast near Prince Rupert)', from the term for 'downriver' (the way by which the north coast is reached). One term does appear to be a loan from Wakashan, however, namely *ʔatl's* 'interior' (cf. Wakashan *'atl-*). The northeast wind *sps* is isolated, but the west wind *tcalsqalh* (from *tca-* 'area' and *ʔasqa* 'outside') presumably refers specifically to the coast to the west.

wind directions, most using directional suffixes on the base *yu-* 'blow', can be gleaned from the dictionaries of Lincoln and Rath, and are generally predictable from the semantics ('up/down inlet', etc.),[23] but some of the more opaque wind terms come from directions somewhat skewed when compared to their use in Kwak'wala – thus southeast *młas* is replaced by related *młuyala* from the northeast. Note also north or out-from-inlet wind *gayuyala* corresponding to *yuya* mentioned above for Kingcome Inlet (but probably containing *gay-* 'starting point' and *-uya-* 'out', as also the preceding item).

Finally, the same basic system has been carried as far north as Kitimat, where Haisla speakers still live today, far inland up Douglas Channel. Like in neighbouring inland Tsimshianic, the system here is almost fully riverine, with no ambiguity at Kitimat as far as the 'downstream' vs. 'upstream' terms are concerned.[24] This is no doubt facilitated by the fact that 'north/south' in the broader geographical sense happens to coincide here rather well with the axis of the inlet. The natural etymological link between *n'ala-* and the south ('daylight)' is completely severed, however: *n'ala-* is now suddenly 'north' (upstream), a sure sign that the system did not originate here. There is another, more transparent term for 'north', namely *t'nsk'utmiʔ,* based on *t'n-* 'cold' and *-k'ut* 'side'. Again like in Tsimshianic, the system is so closely geared to the linear north/south axis that reference to 'east' and 'west' are not so often or so unambiguously distinguished, although *'atl-* 'landward' and *tl'as-* 'seaward' can indeed be used this way, since the Pacific does still lie (far) to the west, as in Heiltsuk. The 'landward' (east) and the 'seaward' (west) side of both the house and the inlet are distinguished this way, and the people from Kitlope/Kemano, lying on an orthogonal side inlet to Douglas Channel (Gardner Canal), are called *'atl'asamXi* 'inland people' from the viewpoint of Kitimat (to their northwest). The expected terms are used for

23. The same suffixes can be added to *la-* 'go', *gaX-* 'come' or "empty" root *'u-* to produce many specific combinations, as for example Heiltsuk *'uwił* 'inlet', *'uy'uatli* 'centre of passage in water', *'uy'uis* 'centre of lake, bay or inlet', *'uq^{w}ia* 'head of inlet', or Haisla *laXan'uisa* 'go to the waterline', *lagl'a* 'go ashore', and *laksiwis* 'go through passage (of water)'.

24. There is a conflict, however, between the (north)west wind term *Xay'utl'(la)* and *Xaʔis* 'downriver', which share the same root, as also in Heiltsuk. Note that the name Haisla derives from this root, which may seem surprising for the northernmost Wakashan language (and village), lying far upstream, but there may be a local explanation: Emmon Bach (pers. comm.) points out that the present village of Haisla is actually downstream from Kitimat and the upper reaches of the river entering Douglas Channel from the north.

going down and up inlet (*la-tus* vs. *la-la*), and these are also used at Kitlope, so that a journey from Kitimat to Kitlope (or vice versa) would combine two stages describable by the two terms respectively (though it is also possible to use *'awitl* 'go inland' of going from Kitimat to Kitlope). These terms and the corresponding directional stems *Xaʔis* (as in *XaXisaqla* 'travel downriver') and *n'ala-* (as in *n'alaqa* '(move) further upstream') must thus be ambivalent at Kitlope as between the local sense ('east' vs. 'west') along Gardner Canal and the broader regional sense, 'north' vs. 'south', as at Kitimat, although, as usual, context doubtless disambiguates in most communicative situations.

3. Tsimshianic: riverine and coastal

The orientation systems of the Tsimshianic languages are fairly uniform and similar in turn to the Tlingit system and the Haisla variant of the Northern Wakashan one, i.e. quintessentially riverine, with 'north/south' aligning with 'upriver/downriver'. They are simpler than the Northern Wakashan system we have looked at, since they lack the paired lexical suffixes going with the directional stems there, though they do display a wide array of proclitics of a spatial nature comparable with the Wakashan lexical suffixes. As can be seen on Map 3 the basic axis is supplemented by a large number of specific wind terms, based in part on spatial proclitics.[25] As with Northern Wakashan, however, ambiguity (or rather vagueness) can occur within Coast Tsimshian, where the major rivers and inlets meet the Pacific. The influence of English cardinal directions may be felt, as elsewhere, in the interpretation of some of these terms today.

The most straightforward – and probably original – system is that displayed by inland Nisga'a (also written Nishga) and closely related Gitksan (GitsenimX or GitksanimX). The basic opposition here is upstream *q'ali-* vs. downstream *gisi-/g^yisi-* (I cite proclitics like these with a following hyphen though they are words in their own right). These – and associated locational terms *ge'ets* and *gigeenix* – correlate fairly well with cardinal south and north (e.g. in translation from English), and are also used of 'up/down inlet' in the coast language. The Nass and the Skeena valleys do indeed turn northwards further inland from the coast. Tarpent (1987) gives a considerable number of other spatial proclitics expressing such meanings as 'down to the river ' *(y'aqa-)* 'up from the river' (*paX-*), 'across the river' (*caqa-*), 'in to shore' (*caqam-*), 'out from shore' *('uk^ws-*), 'emerging from woods, back from woods' (*n'aa-*), 'along the shoreline' (*hał-*), 'around back of houses/village, into woods' (*q'altix-*), etc., most of which have exact counterparts in Coast Tsimshian. Wind terms may also contain proclitics, e.g. *luu-ba'ask^w*, a southwestern wind up the Nass, based on *luu-* 'inside'

25. Pure directions may sometimes be distinguished from wind terms by the addition of a proclitic, *n'atXa-* 'in such and such a direction' in Coast Tsimshian (thus *n'atXag^yisiyaask* 'north' as opposed to *g^yisiyaask* 'north wind'), or by *anuu/an-* in the inland languages (as in the phrasal directionals discussed below).

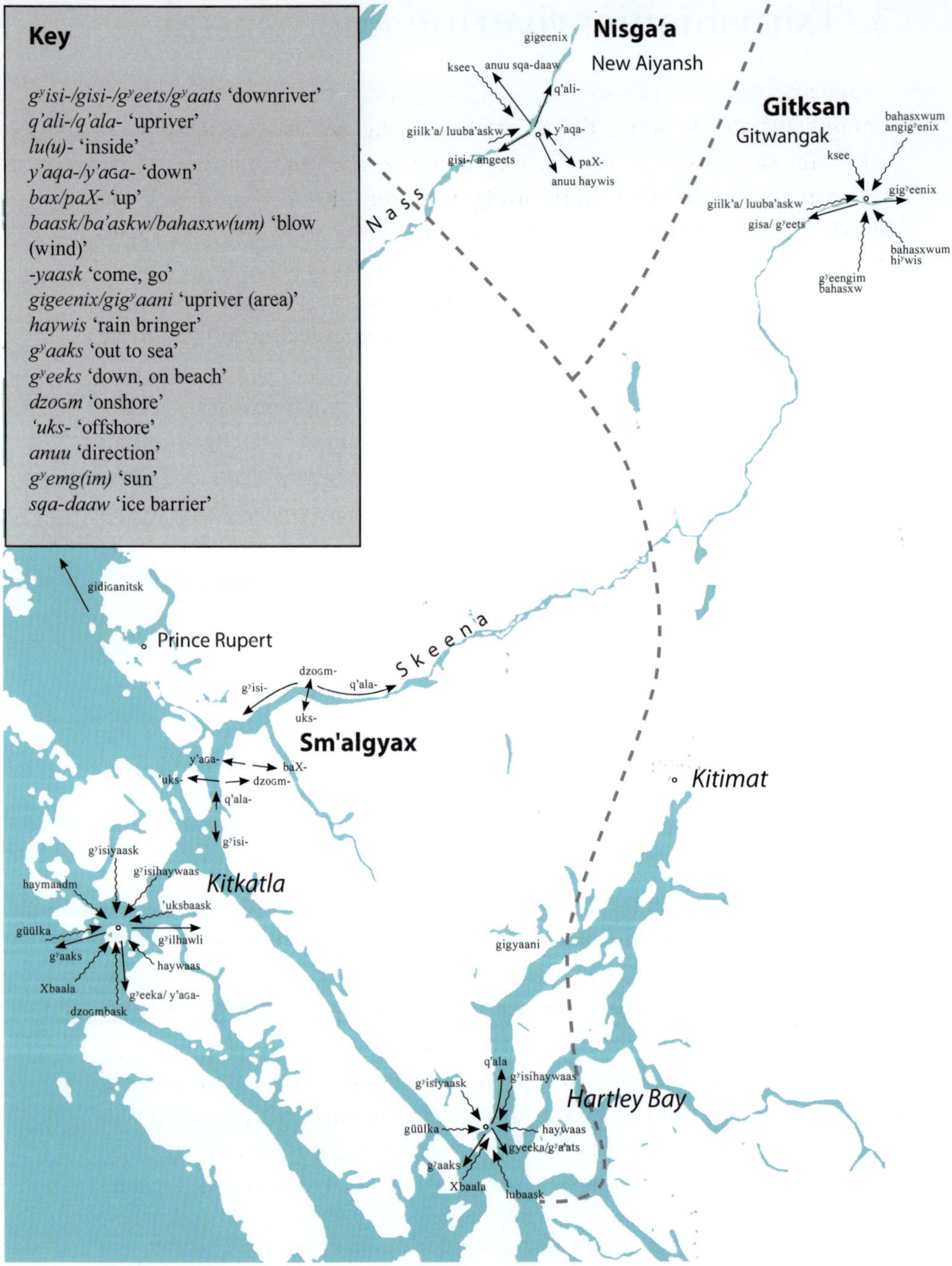

Map 3 Tsimshianic.

and *ba'ask*^{w} 'blowing' of a wind (which has a counterpart in Gitksan referring to the Skeena).

Superimposed on this axis in both Nisga'a and Gitksan are east/west phrases glossable as 'where the sun rises/sets', e.g. *wil luu-daaw'ił łoqs* 'west, where the sun goes in' in Nisga'a. Similar phrases are found to express wider geographical 'north' and 'south' using *anuu* 'direction of', as in *anuu sqadaaw* (literally 'in the direction where ice blocks the way') and *anuu haywis* 'in the direction of the southerly rain'. These may or may not be influenced by the need to translate English cardinal directions. In Gitksan these north/south terms are represented by *anuu ksee* 'direction of the north wind' (this wind is also found in Nisga'a) and *g*^{y}*emgim bahask*^{w} (lit. 'hot wind', from *g*^{y}*emk* 'warmth, sun'). There are slight differences in eastern Gitksan at Kispiox (Bruce Rigsby, pers. comm.), but the semantics of the terms are the same. There are, as to be expected, no terms specific to up/down the coast of British Columbia, although Rigsby does give *anuu laX mo'on* 'coastward' for Kispiox (more specifically 'towards the inner tidal sheltered waters') and the corresponding wind *bahasxum laX mo'on* 'west wind'.

The situation in Coast Tsimshian (nowadays called Sm'algyax, a term once used of the whole family acc. Rigsby, pers. comm.) is, hardly surprisingly, more directly relatable to the coast – which, it should be noted, is highly indented, with many islands, inlets and channels, as elsewhere on the Northwest Coast. It looks, in fact, as if the riverine system of Nisga'a and Gitksan was adapted to the coast at some point, resulting in the ambivalence of a number of the originally riverine terms, since the rivers typically come out at the coast from cardinal east rather than from the north. This is particularly evident as regards the 'downriver' term *g*^{y}*isi-*, which is associated on the coast with 'north', as in *g*^{y}*isi-yaask*, everywhere a north wind, i.e. blowing downriver from the north (*yaask* is an "anti-passive" form of *yaa* 'go, come') – though it can still retain its easterly sense at Kitkatla (on a small island off the mainland south of larger Porcher Island) when referring to the wind down the Skeena. This is an areal feature shared with neighbouring Haisla and Tlingit. The opposite term for 'upriver' (*q'ala-*) is not used to refer to the south in this way, however (i.e. as constant wind source) – the adaptation of the riverine terms to the coast is evidently not everywhere complete. Note that I have added these terms plus the 'out onto the water' and 'in to the shore' proclitics rather arbitrarily on the lower Skeena river, since these senses of the words are recognized everywhere.

On the shore between the mouth of the river and Kitkatla I have indicated the coastally reinterpreted orientation of these 'upriver/downriver' items (also proclitics *y'aGa-* 'down to shore' and *baX-* 'up from shore', which are the same everywhere in their local senses). At Kitkatla they also have a larger areal sense of 'coming up from the south' (*baX-baa*) and the opposite (*y'aGa-baa*), at loggerheads with the usual local sense, as in *baX-yaa* 'walk up from the beach' and *y'aGa-yaa* 'walk down to the beach'. Also *dzoGam-baa* 'go to(wards) the shore' in Kitkatla has a wider geographical sense, namely to go to Prince Rupert (on the mainland opposite), as opposed to *wul(a)m-baa*, which everywhere only has the local meaning of 'come to shore'. Note that 'upriver' term *q'ala-* is consequently used aṭ Kitkatla (as in *q'ala-baa* with *baa* 'go, run') about going up the channel towards the mouth of the Skeena, but *also* about going up the Skeena itself (and the converse as regards *gʸisi-baa*). As with the inland languages, there are also phrases for 'where the sun rises/sets' for east and west, used in a non-ambiguous manner, namely *wilmanyaa-gʸemk* and *wiltkiyaa-gʸemk* respectively.

There is a certain degree of variation in wind terms according to locality – as stated, these constitute a major source of directional terms in Tsimshianic apart from the 'upriver/downriver' ones. Thus the wind roses I have elicited for the two villages where the language is still used on a daily basis, Kitkatala and Hartley Bay (on the mainland to the south), differ somewhat.[26] Most of the terms employed are recognizable from the inland languages, although those that contain proclitics referring to 'out to sea' or its opposite 'landward' vary predictably according to locality (the village of Hartley Bay is east-facing, Kitkatla north-facing). Thus *dzoGm-baask* 'onshore wind' is from the east at Hartley Bay but from the open sea to the south at Kitkatla (not from the north, where only a narrow channel separates it from Porcher Island). Others, such as *haywaas* from the southeast (literally 'rain bringer', corresponding to Nisga'a *haywis*), *Xbaala* 'southwest wind', and the bitterly cold *gʸisi-haywaas* from the northeast (cf. the 'downriver' sense of *gʸisi-*) are from the same direction everywhere (though *Xbaala* is described as 'mild' at Kitkatla but glossed as 'storm from the south' by Dunn[27]). Other impor-

26. I have no information about the state of the (coastal) language spoken at Metlakatla, Alaska, where a small community moved in the last century. Apparently few people if anyone speaks the language there today. Dunn has *gʸisiyaask* 'north' vs. *gʸe'ets* 'south' for there, which is what one expects from usage further south. Note the etymology of the name given by Boas: maXłə-*qaala*, lit. 'narrow channel of sea' from proclitic *maXłə-* 'through a narrow channel).

27. In such forms cited from Dunn I do not distinguish ordinary and capital 'a' (the latter as in the last syllable of *Xbaala*, which could be represented by schwa as in Boas, or, as in other sources, underlined 'a'). Note in Sasama (2001) the proclitic *Xbal-* 'up, northwards'

tant winds in the coastal language are *haymaadm* 'west (or northwest) wind in winter' (literally 'snow bringer') and *gűűlka* 'west wind (summer only)' (probably the same as *giilk'a* mentioned by Tarpent for Nisga'a as a gentle west wind). Dunn also has for Hartley Bay *yüksmoots* '(south)east wind in autumn (bringing rainstorm)' and *XsooGmlaXay'ans* 'strong north wind at beginning of winter' (probably from *ksoo* 'frost' – cf. Nisga'a *ksee*?). Particular to Kitkatla is *g^yilmiyaansk* 'south wind'– cf. the first element of *g^yilhawli* 'up into the woods (behind the village)'.[28]

There are also the words *g^ya'aks* 'out to sea' (cf. proclitic *'uks-*) and *g^ye'ets* (or *g^ya'ats*) literally 'down below', referring respectively to the west and south in a general way, the second one found also in Nisga'a and Gitksan in its 'downriver' (and hence roughly 'south') sense. At Hartley Bay *g^yaaks* is used in a wider geographical sense of 'towards Kitkatla' (as well as locally 'out of the strait to sea'). Note also *g^yeeka/g^yiika*, literally 'down on the beach'.[29] We have here a further piece of evidence for the adaptation of an original riverine system to the coast in Coast Tsimshian, a 'downriver' term having become 'south down coast'. This is particularly clear at Kitkatla, where *g^yi-g^yaani* 'upriver' can also mean north up the channel to Prince Rupert (as well as up the small inlet on nearby Porcher Island). In general, the channel between it and Porcher Island is apparently conceptualized as an extension out to sea of the Skeena river, and something similar can be said of the channel leading out to sea to the southwest of Hartley Bay, i.e. as an extension of Douglas Inlet, which leads upriver to Kitimat (which is in fact called *G^yig^yaani* in Hartley Bay).

However, speakers seem in general unwilling to use their 'upriver/downriver' terms over larger geographical areas along the coast (e.g. between their village and Prince Rupert), preferring to spell out the names of the starting point and destination (similar remarks were made by Kwak'wala speakers). Thus *g^yisi-* would not readily be used to refer to traveling towards Alaska (the source of the northern wind), although there is a wind name with that

(e.g. from Hartley Bay towards Prince Rupert). She also gives the opposite: *tgi-/tk^yi-* 'down, down south'.

28. Also in a broader geographical sense 'way up inland, to the east'. Dunn erroneously gives *g^yil-* as an 'upriver' proclitic. For the second part of the 'south wind' term compare *miyaansda*, used of the south at Kitkatla.

29. At Kitkatla *g^ya'ats* has the special meaning of 'east (end of town)', probably because it is in that direction the narrow channel on its north side emerges into the broader north/south orientated inlet to the east (Dunn has *n'atXag^ya'ats* 'into inland').

proclitic, *g^{y}isaGaniitsk* (a variant of *g^{y}idaGaniitsk*) referring to the northwest wind from the direction of the Tlingits – or to the Tlingits themselves.

Finally, it should be pointed out that Tsimshianic languages do not apply "macrocosmic" geographical directionals to the interior of the house as in Northern Wakashan and Tlingit, although it does have proclitics specifically indicating motion towards the walls from the centre of the house (the fireplace in the traditional house) and the reverse, i.e. *laGauk-* 'from side of house to the fire' and *ts'ək'ał-* 'from fire to the side of the house' (the forms given by Boas 1911 for Coast Tsimshian).[30] Nor are the words for 'left side' and 'right side' applied to objects as opposed to the human body. Among its many spatial proclitics, however, Nisga'a also has *y'aws-* 'from a confined or hidden place into the open' and its opposite, *kic'ił-* 'into a confined or hidden place (e.g. between village and woods)', which can be compared to the terms *q'ad(a)* and *diid(a)* forming a similar (and most important) axis in Haida, to be described in the following section.

30. I could not re-elicit these. Boas also gives *asdi-* 'from the middle to the front of the house, back from fire' – acc. Tarpent (pers. comm.) 'off to the side' rather; *wuts'ən-* 'along through middle, back through house to rear'; *Gami-* 'to rear of house' (cf. Nisga'a *kimi-* 'at the rear (e.g. of house)'); and *t'əm-* 'from rear to middle of house' (in Nisga'a 'away from, esp. from wall towards middle of house' acc. Tarpent).

4. Haida: an isolated "large island" system

Haida, spoken out on the Queen Charlotte Islands (which effectively form one large island split across the middle), is linguistically an isolate, although its speakers in the past were highly mobile travellers up and down the Northwest coast. Its orientation system is rather different from that of its mainland neighbours, though it shares many basic parameters with them. It is quintessentially maritime, with *q'ad*(a) 'out to sea' (and by extension 'down to the beach') vs. *diid*(a) 'landwards' (and by extension 'up from the beach into woods') forming the major orientation axis. Enrico (2005) has a somewhat more abstract opposition, one we have already seen in Nisga'a on the mainland and will see again in Tlingit, namely 'towards an open space / in a clear space' vs. 'towards a closed space / at the edge of a clear space', which covers other senses than the purely maritime – including the domestic. Applied to the immediate vicinity of the house (*nee*) Enrico has (for Masset) *nee didgu* 'behind the house', *nee q'adgu* 'in front of the house'.

Corresponding to these directional noun stems are two (unrelated) suffixes, *-s(G)a* and *-gał / -gił*, which necessarily shift direction around the coast of the island(s), just as the 'down there' vs. 'up there' demonstratives in coastal Eskimo do. I have designated this "large island" system as a fifth major subtype in the region although one could regard it simply as a variant of the general coastal type alongside the purely coast-relative (e.g. maritime Eskimo), and archipelagoan (e.g. Aleut) ones. However, terms with the dedicated 'left along coast' vs. 'right along coast' meanings of coastal Eskimo are not found, nor is there clear evidence of origins in a riverine system, as is the case in Kodiak Island Alutiiq. There is no reference to landmarks on the mainland in the core system, nor is there ambivalence between the microcosmic and the macrocosmic use of the same terms (with two local exceptions – see below concerning the vicinities of Masset and Hydaburg).

Wind terms play an important role. As can be seen on Map 4, they are partially uniform in absolute direction across the islands and the three main dialect areas (including Alaskan Haida on Prince of Wales Island, to which some northern – Masset – Haida moved in the early 18th century). The wind *xiw* (with uvular /X/ in Skidegate, a pharyngeal trill in Masset) is, for example,

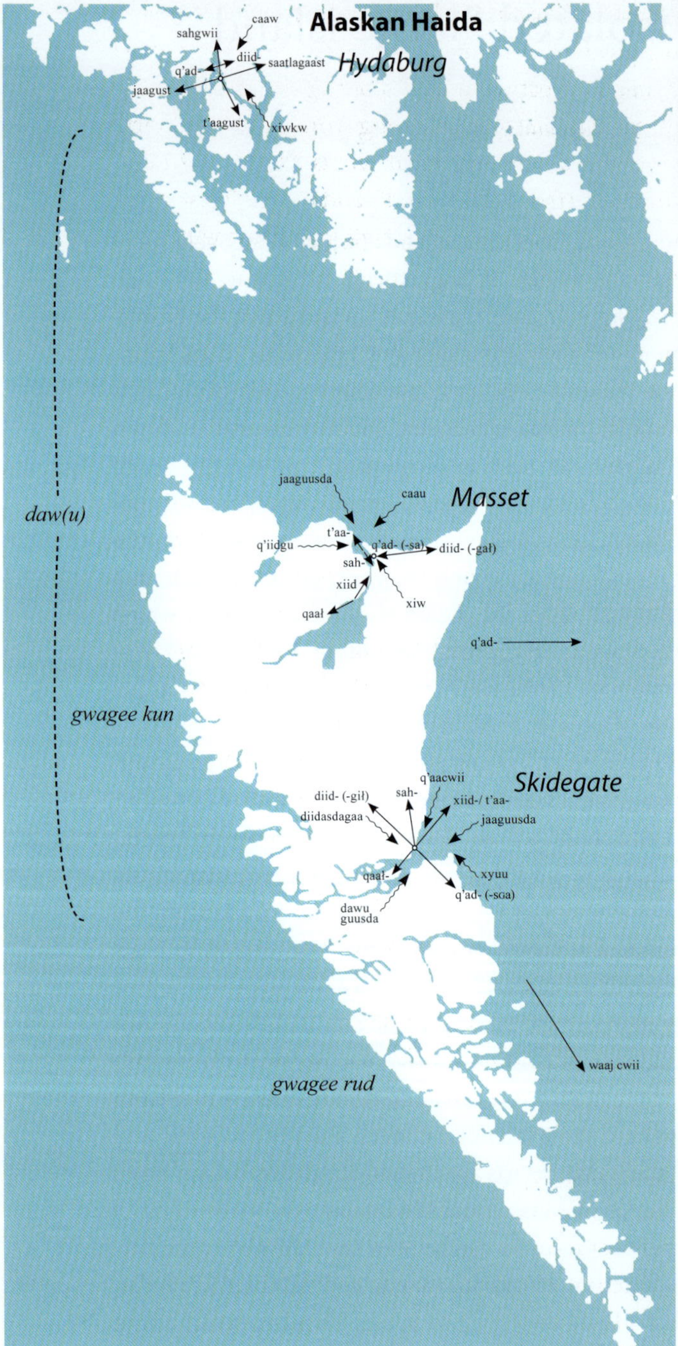

Key

q'ad-/-sGa-/-sa 'towards open place, down on beach, on ocean'
diid-/-gał/-gił 'towards edge of open place (up on land, behind house)'
qaał 'up inlet (inside area)'
sah- 'above, up inlet'
q'iid 'strait'
xiid- 'down'
jaa 'mouth of inlet or channel'
t'aa 'mouth of inlet'
daw(u) 'side'
-guusda/-guust 'from a direction'
-gwaa/gwii/cwii 'short way in a direction'

Map 4 Haida.

everywhere from the southeast, and *caau* (with palato-velar /ç/) 'northeast' is the same at Masset and Hydaburg at least.[31] Others are by necessity more local, such as Skidegate *tajuu-sGa* 'west wind' (lit. 'blowing towards the sea'), which corresponds to Masset *tajuu-saa(gaa)* ('blowing from land' – i.e. north out of the inlet). There are also some very local winds like Masset *tlagas kuunsda* 'north wind in summer' (from *tlaga* 'land') and *q'iidgu* 'west wind' (from *q'iid* 'strait, channel'),[32] and Skidegate *q'aa cwii* 'northeast wind' and *q'ang* 'moderate southeast wind in summer'.

There is a difference between local and broader regional interpretations of the key terms, as in many other areas, and at Masset (that is, the new town) this results in actual ambivalence of one of the central terms (although, as usual, context distinguishes): the 'down to the beach' sense of *q'ad* at Masset points roughly west, whereas the broader 'out to the open sea' sense points towards the mainland to the east (around Prince Rupert).[33] Enrico specifies the range of the 'down to beach from house' sense of *q'ad* here as no more than 100 feet (op. cit.: 1489). This no doubt reflects the movement of the new town up Masset Inlet from the old village (Old Masset at the mouth of the inlet on the coast). Houses at both sites would have faced the water (as they still do). At Skidegate, facing out to sea, this ambiguity does not arise.

Perhaps more important than wind directions in the Haida orientation system are its 'up inlet/channel' vs. 'down inlet/channel' terms, notably *qaał* vs. *xiid*(a) (literally 'inside area' and 'down' respectively – note once again the parallel to the coastal Eskimo axis already mentioned in connection with Southern Wakashan). The actual orientations of these directions are highly dependent on local setting. At Masset also *sah* vs. *t'aa* (literally 'up' vs. 'foot end, mouth of') have these opposing meanings, only at a shorter range, near the mouth of the inlet. These may refer locally to 'south' vs. 'north', as at Masset (where Masset Sound plus Inlet could be described as a south-going river plus a lake at its end) and in Alaskan Haida (where the main channel is oriented north/south, the mirror image of at Masset), while at Skidegate

31. Related to Tlingit *xûn* 'north wind' acc. Enrico, so perhaps a loan – Lawrence (1997) has *xaakw* (with velar /x/) for Hydaburg. Note that I keep Lawrence's orthographical conventions for Alaskan Haida on the map (otherwise I follow Enrico's).
32. The element *-gu* is just 'at'. The same stem can be seen in the Masset term for the Alaskan Haida, *q'iis xaadee*, named after Langara Island off the NW coast of Graham Island where the Alaskan Haida initially moved.
33. Thus the Masset word for 'mainland' *q'adgwaa gwaayee* (Skidegate *q'ada-cwaa gwaayaay*), where the second word means 'island'.

(situated at the wider end of Skidegate Channel), the axis is east/west, with the wider east end regarded as the 'mouth' (*jiʔa-/jaa-*). At Masset *qaał gwii* 'up inlet' (with *gwii* 'towards') is also 'towards Skidegate'. Corresponding to these directional stems there are suffixes, namely Masset *-t'ał* 'down inlet' (lit. 'down') and *-ts'a*, Skidegate *-ts'i* 'into inlet (or house)'; note also *-na* 'from land', *-t'as* 'across horizontal expanse (body of water, arm of the sea)', and *-qał* 'from the sea'.

At both Skidegate and Hydaburg (Alaskan Haida) *sah* ('up') has the (natural) meaning of 'north', still opposite to *t'aa* at Hydaburg, though it points out to sea along with *xiid(a)* at Skidegate. In all dialects the latter term has a broader areal sense of 'towards the lower mainland/Puget Sound'. Also t'*aa* 'towards mouth of inlet' may have this broader sense – but *t'aa cwii* means locally 'northwest' at Hydaburg, so there is conflict between the broader and local senses there.[34] Lawrence also has *saa tlagaast* 'east' for Hydaburg (from *sa(h)* 'up' and *tlaga* 'land' – so 'up towards the land'?) as opposed to *jaaguust* 'west', lit. 'up inlet/up channel', which Enrico has as *jaagusd(agaa)* '(wind) blowing from northwest' for Masset (also as a nominal 'West Wind') but 'southeast wind' for Hydaburg. It is naturally from the east at Skidegate. This only makes sense when one notices that there is (narrower) channel mouth (*jaa*) both to the west of Hydaburg and (the main one) to the southeast (where *t'aa* is also used). It is unclear whether these terms given as pure directionals by Lawrence are actually wind terms, glossing the nearest cardinal equivalents in English. The ambivalence of both *sa(h)* and *jaa* could at all events be symptomatic of the recent move of the Alaskan Haida to their present location.

Other important larger scale reference points are *daw(u)/duu* (literally 'side') referring everywhere to the west coast of the Queen Charlotte and Prince of Wales Islands, and the terms *gwaagee rud* and *gwaagee kun* (literally 'rear' and 'front' ends) referring to the south (Moresby) and the north (Graham) island respectively. In Masset *waaj cwii/gwii* (from *waaj* 'over there') refers to the southern mainland (around Puget Sound), while at Skidegate it refers to the southern end of the Queen Charlottes. Note that *q'ad-* has the specific interpretation 'towards the mainland (around Prince Rupert)' at both localities. There are also words for 'across, on opposite side', notably *xanł-* as in *xanł-guusda* 'on the other side from –' (*guusda/cuusda* is 'side').

34. More locally, *t'aa gwaa* at Masset (the new town) may refer to Old Masset at the mouth of the inlet, but also, further afield, continuing out into the strait, it may refer to Langara Island, according to Enrico.

Haida is one of the languages, like Kwak'wala, that display the conflation of the meanings 'out to sea' and 'towards the fireplace (away from the wall)' – and its converse – which will be discussed further in a separate section. Here it is realized in the fact that the 'out to sea / landwards' (*q'ad(a)* vs. *diid(a)*) opposition mentioned earlier also refers respectively to 'towards the fireplace in the centre of the room' and 'away from the fireplace towards the wall'. These are also found in *diidguusda / diidcuusda* 'landward side, back of house (inside), back part of town (towards woods)' and *q'adacuusda*, which in Skidegate is glossed by Enrico as 'at the side nearest clear space' (e.g. the side of the house nearest water – generally the front), and in Masset as 'between X and the fire (only if the fire is in the centre of the room)'. As will be seen, there are notable parallels in Tlingit on the Alaskan mainland.

5. Alaskan Na-Dene

This subject has been treated by Leer, who shows that there is a common "waterway" system shared by all these languages,[35] and I have little to add to his basic analysis. His schematic charts for Tlingit, Eyak and Athabaskan are shown in Figure 2 below. I accept his suggestion (Leer 1989: 602) that the common Na-Dene 'downriver/upriver' terms may in fact have had a more abstract (or general) origin, namely 'in front' vs. 'behind' (while the 'down to water' and 'up from water' terms can be reconstructed as such for Proto-Athabaskan-Eyak at least). However, a number of details as regards more precise geographical settings can be added, and his open question as to whether the original system was riverine or maritime can be addressed in broader areal terms.

Leer did not deal specifically with Dena'ina, the only coastal northern Athabaskan language. Data on this language (based on Kari 2007) can be seen on Map 7 for the Bering Sea area and compared with Leer's schema for general Athabaskan in Figure 2. It will be seen that Dena'ina has a rather simple system of oppositions, similar in essence to that of neighbouring Kenai Peninsula Alutiiq further out along Cook Inlet, both of which appear to represent coastal adaptations of earlier riverine systems. In the case of Dena'ina (as in Alutiiq) this involves the conceptualization of Cook Inlet as a broad river, opening out into the Pacific to the southwest. Thus the 'upriver/downriver' terms on Leer's generalized schema (**niʔ* vs. *daʔ*) correspond to 'up inlet' and 'down inlet' respectively (*nit/-n'ə* vs. *dut/-t'ə*), while the 'upland/downland' ones (**nəG* vs.**cənʔ*) remain the same (respectively *-nggə* vs. *-tsən*, the latter pointing out over the inlet).[36] Considerably more variation

35. This covers Athabaskan-Eyak, including the southern Apachean and California/Oregon branches, which Leer also briefly discusses. Eyak is a distant outlier to Athabaskan and Tlingit is much more remotely related. Note that Haida, regarded by Sapir as related to this family, is now generally believed to be an isolate.

36. These directions are also applied to the house: *nggə* can also be 'towards the rear wall' and *tsən* 'towards the front wall. Compare also Koyukon *naa/n'e/nee* 'upstream, in back of house', *do'u* 'downstream', *negge* 'upland, from water, toward rear wall', *tlen* 'downland, toward water, toward front wall', also *nete* 'in front, towards perimeter', and *'en* 'out in the open, off'. The fact that Koyukon (unlike Dena'ina) conflates 'back of house' and 'upstream' (like Central Alaskan Yupik) will be returned to in the section on Fire and Water.

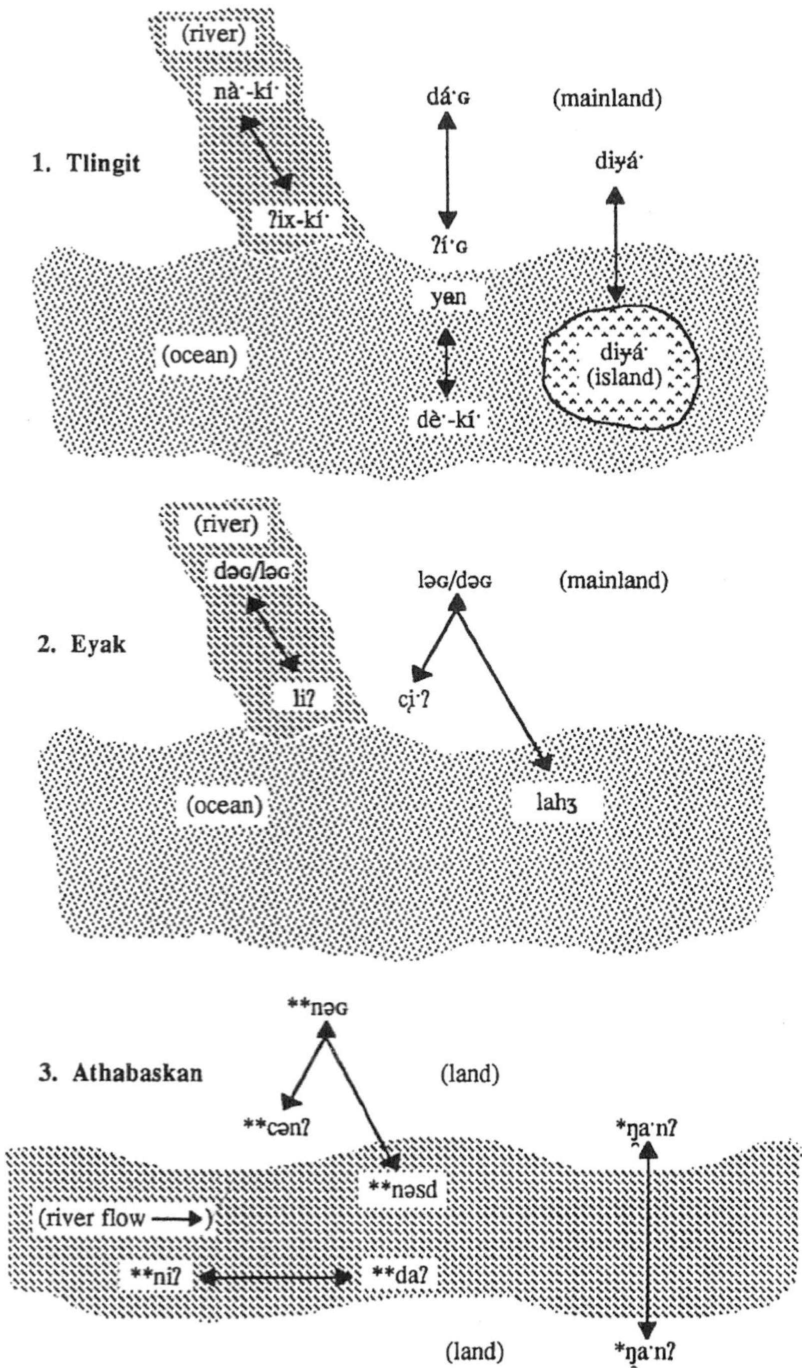

Fig. 2 Na-Dene waterway-oriented directionals (Leer 1989).

enters the picture when one looks at wind directions (not discussed by Leer). Kari gives information for a number of different sites. For Tyonek on the northwest shore of mid-Cook Inlet there is, for example (like for Alutiiq further south), a southwest 'up inlet' wind (*yuuduch'*) and a southeast 'from across the inlet' one (*ts'inuni*), both etymologically transparent.[37] Terms for winds from these directions are quite different at inland sites such as at Nondalton, north of Lake Iliamna, where the northeast wind is *dunidi* (literally 'from upriver', along Lake Clark) and the southwest wind is *duduch'* (lit. 'from downstream', where Lake Clark empties into Iliamna Lake).

Outside of the basic set of orthogonal axes discussed so far – and forming, rather, a separate opposition with **nəG* – is **nəsd* on Leer's schema, which is glossed by him as 'ahead'. In Lower Tanana its reflex *nətha* refers to 'off from shore, into fire', one of the sporadic attestations of that conflation of meanings in Athabaskan languages to be discussed in the section on Fire and Water. The corresponding term in Dena'ina is *nus/yus/dus*, which contains distinct prefixes (cf. *du-* 'near' and *yu-* 'far') and which Kari (pers. comm.) glosses variously as 'at (the outer) perimeter, out to sea, in front, by the fire, into the open'.[38] One wonders whether the "missing" opposite of **nəsd* did not have the converse 'up from the water, away from the fire' sense found in Tlingit and Haida equivalents (and in Koyukon prefix string *nee-gho-*). Dena'ina also has a reflex of Leer's reconstructed 'across' directional **ŋa·nʔ* (e.g. in the second half of *ts'inuni* 'straight across', already mentioned as a wind term).

As regards Tlingit, we can already see in Leer's schema the result of an essentially riverine system coming down to the ocean, namely the 'upriver/downriver' axis (*na·-* vs. *ʔix-*) coming to align itself with the coast ('north' vs. 'south' respectively) while remaining orthogonal to the 'upland/downland' one (this is not so apparent on the schema, but should be clearer on Map 5). As it happens the long inlets of the coastal Tlingit region do align themselves roughly north/south (i.e. the 'upstream' end lies naturally to the north). Note that there are distinct 'out from the shore/into shore' and 'up into the land/down to the shore' oppositions, as in all coastally adapted

37. The Dena'ina refer in fact to the Kenai Peninsula Alutiit as *dutna* 'down inlet people'.
38. He contrasts this with *ʔənə* 'outside, off, away', which refers in the wider sense to "alien" territory, beyond the perimeter, as opposed to **nəsd* 'out to the perimeter (of territory)' – note the derivative of the latter in both Dena'ina and Ahtna *dənsə* (containing **nəsd*) refers to the southwest, in the case of (inland) Ahtna 'over the Chugach mountains, Prince William Sound' (compare Eyak *lahz* 'out to sea, south' below).

systems in this survey except Dena'ina (where the 'upland' term – *nəggəch'* – does the service of 'ashore'). The 'up from the shore' and 'out to sea' opposition is of particular importance: *da·G* (from **dəG*) covers 'towards the interior, back away from an open area, towards the woods, back from the centre of the main living area, away from the fire', as well as 'up from the shore', and *da·g* is 'into the open, towards the centre of the main living area, into the fire' as well as 'out to sea from the shore'.[39] The 'down to the shore, downland' term *ʔi·G* is cognate with Athabaskan-Eyak *yəX* 'down', while the 'in to shore' one, *ÿan*, apparently lacks a cognate in the other languages (it also means 'to completion, finishing'). There is also an 'across to other side' term, *diÿa·*, apparently cognate with the Athabaskan form mentioned above (/ÿ/ is an unrounded high back semivowel).

I have added further detail for Tlingit on Map 5, namely some relevant wind terms for the central dialect area around Juneau (the 'east' and 'west' ones are related to the 'upland' vs. 'downland' directionals respectively), plus information on their somewhat different orientation at Sitka (according to Wrangell 1839) and on the Stikine River (according to Boas 1891) – note that the different (more or less east/west) orientation of the river in the latter case explains the skewing of all but the 'north' wind. The wind *yande-at* is an onshore wind, based on directional *ÿan* 'towards shore'. (Note that I have adjusted Wrangell's and Boas' spellings somewhat, but maintained the orthographical conventions of newer sources.) All of these areas belong to the main northern dialect area (dialect differences within Tlingit are concentrated in the far south).

I have also added relevant terms for Interior Tlingit from Leer et al. (2001). This has been somewhat simplified, since there are differences in the various locations (Atlin, Carcross and Teslin) to which the Taku River Tlingit moved inland within the last two centuries. Note that Leer's claim (1989: 586) that Interior Tlingit has adjusted the original 'upland/downland' terms to refer now to 'upriver/downriver' is not repeated in the 2001 dictionary, probably because this reinterpretation does not apply in the same way to the whole inland region now occupied by Interior Tlingit speakers (along lakes and rivers no longer necessarily orientated north/south). Thus the 'south' wind *sanaxh-at* at Atlin (which is still on a north/south lake axis) is actually an east

39. The form *de·ki* is a fossilized combination of the directional stem plus a following head *ki·*, which may be cognate with *ki·* 'up' according to Leer. Note too the locational derivatives *digina* referring to the front room, as opposed to *daGina*, referring to the back room of the house.

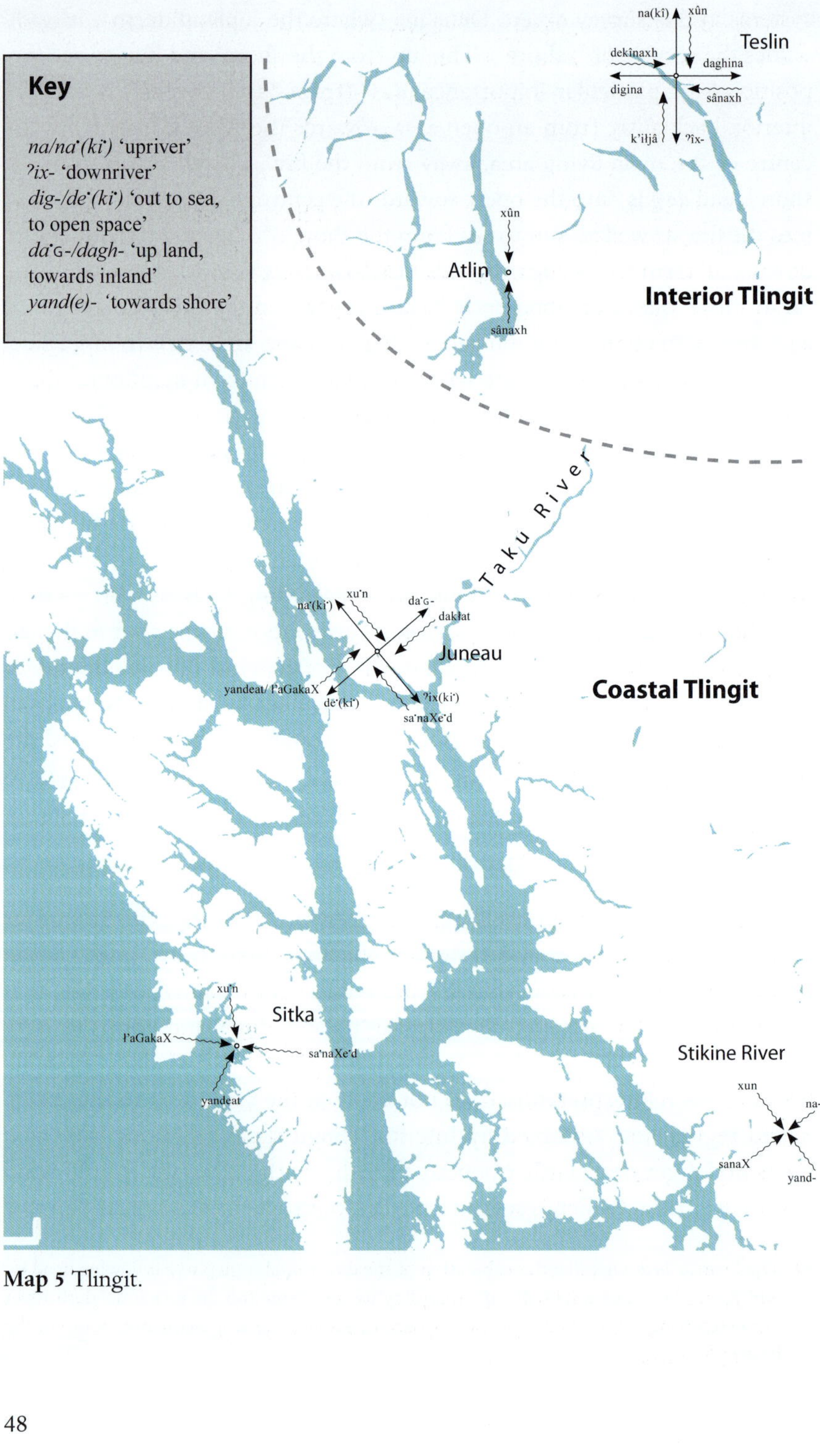

Map 5 Tlingit.

wind at other Interior Tlingit sites (*sânaxh*). The overall situation suggests a rather recent breakdown of the 'north/upriver' vs. 'south/downriver' axis central to coastal Tlingit as these groups moved inland, this opposition now referring mainly to cardinal 'north' vs. 'south', as Leer points out.[40]

As I have stated in the Introduction, this does not mean that the coastal Tlingit system from which the Interior one developed has always been a coastal one. In fact the orthogonally "ambiguous" nature of the two crossing axes, with 'upriver' either referring to literally 'upriver' (or 'up inlet') – regardless of the exact orientation of the waterway – or to cardinal 'north' (an areal trait shared with Tsimshianic and Northern Wakashan), is what we now can expect of original riverine systems that have come down to the coast. This suggests an answer to Leer's query: the Tlingit system surely came from inland at some distant time, and was originally riverine, like the Athabaskan languages it split off from.[41] Perhaps the fact that its interior, riverine origins have remained in evidence so long can be attributed in part to the complex coastal geography in southeast Alaska, with its many parallel channels, inlets and large islands producing a landscape that is as much riverine as it is coastal.

The situation in now extinct Eyak (which is assumed by specialists to have come down to the coast, splitting off and becoming isolated from Athabaskan already in ancient times) is more obscure, although it shares much in common with other Na-Dene languages. Thus the upland/downland dimension is expressed with cognate terms in Athabaskan, namely 'upland' *ləG* or *dəG* (going with Athabaskan **nəG* 'upland' and Tlingit *da·G* 'towards the interior' respectively), and 'downland' *ci·ʔ* (going with Athabaskan **cən*ʔ). Also Athabaskan **nəsd* 'out to sea' has its counterpart in *lahz* 'forward, out to sea' (the cognate of Tlingit *ʔix-* 'downstream, south', acc. Leer).[42] The riverine

40. Interior Tlingit also appears here to have an interesting "double" lefthand/righthand distinction, namely between "ordinary" *s'at'naxha* 'area towards left' and *shiynaxha* 'area towards right' (both with stem *naxha* for area in a direction), as opposed to "high language" *łkhaxhênaxha* and *ghayênaxha* respectively. The latter pair would presumably have been used in a ceremonial context, referring to the sides of the house seen from some particular perspective, much as in Kwak'wala (I have no further information on this for interior or coastal Tlingit). Nowhere in Na-Dene do objects appear to have intrinsic left and right sides, however.
41. Carlson (1996: 68) suggests on archaeological grounds a date somewhere between 2,500 and 1,500 years ago for this event. The descent to the coast would, on the linguistic grounds mentioned, probably have occurred at the southern end of their present extent.
42. Krauss has *ʔį·ziʔX k'u·y* 'southerly wind' (Leer 'south') from an irregular allomorph of the same base. He also gives *yahd* 'south, away from shore, out to sea, towards Seattle', and *yəq* 'ashore'.

'upriver/downriver' dimension on the other hand is, as elsewhere, central, but the terms used for them are paradoxical, as both Krauss and Leer have pointed out. That is because although *dəG/ləG* are also used for 'upstream', the opposite, *liʔ* 'downstream', is apparently cognate with Athabaskan *niʔ* 'upstream' (Tlingit *na·*-). Krauss in his dictionary (1970: 454) speculates as to whether this might reflect the inland origin of the Eyak, if for instance they once lived further up the Copper River valley behind the Chugach Range mountains, the narrowing canyon here acting as a natural barrier to movement downstream (he gives the precise gloss of *liʔ* as 'behind, inside, into confined place' as well as 'downriver, towards coast/Gulf'). Leer supports this by adducing the term for the Eyak used by their Ahtna neighbours to the north, namely *danGene* 'upland people'. This would only make sense if the Eyak were once 'upland' from the Ahtna – which they would have been along the Chitina valley for instance, a mountain-encircled *cul-de-sac* off the mid Copper River valley, the source of valuable surface copper (though they could have come to the coast by other routes).

East/west terms are more haphazard (and sometimes explained in a contradictory fashion by different consultants in Krauss' data), thus *yəX* 'down' is glossed variously by Krauss as 'southeast' or 'southwest' as well as 'north' in derivatives like *yəXeʔX k'u·y* 'southeast/southwest wind' (*k'u·y* is 'wind'), *yəXeʔd* 'northwest-ward', *yəXeʔX* 'west', and *yəXʔiłč'ač'* 'towards the northwest – e.g. from Yakutat to Cordova'. I interpret this to mean that *yəXeʔX k'u·y* is essentially a southeast wind (i.e. blowing from the southeast). The term he gives as 'west wind' (i.e. blowing towards the east), *šį·daʔ k'u·y*, is explained as 'up creek' from *šį·* 'stream' plus *daʔ* 'in front'[43] (it is variously glossed as 'to or up creek, northeast, east, southwest, west' with the comment that most streams flow south(west)/west into the Gulf of Alaska). Only one wind term is consistently orientated, namely *Xa·*'north wind'. At all events, the crossing axis is the roughly east/west coastline. As Krauss puts it in discussing wind terms (1970: 270): "The basic orientation is apparently the coastline from Cordova to Yakutat … and the mountain range behind it." The Eyak system (in so far as it survived) was as a whole clearly riverine in origin, with at least one of its 'downland' terms, *yəX* 'down', having received a coastal interpretation in some of its derivatives. However, one does

43. Also (and originally, acc. M. Krauss, pers. comm.) 'arriving at'; cognate with proto-Athabaskan *daʔ* 'downstream' acc. Leer, and ultimately meaning 'lips, outside of the mouth' and as a prefix 'towards the entrance'.

not find the simple application of 'up/downriver' terms to up and down the coast as one does in Tlingit and Dena'ina – this is no doubt because the idiosyncratic development of the original 'up/downriver' terms had already occurred in the language well before its speakers (who never truly adapted to a seafaring way of life) came down to the coast.

A plausible overall scenario for what might have happened with Eyak on its way towards the coast is as follows. It relies on Leer's reconstruction of the Proto-Athabaskan-Eyak *niʔ* vs. *daʔ* axis as originally 'behind' vs. 'in front' (and only secondarily 'upriver' vs. 'downriver'), and presupposes the reanalysis not only of these terms as 'upriver/downriver' (with ultimately different results in the two branches of the family) but also on the concomitant replacement of the original 'behind/in front' opposition by another axis in Eyak, namely its 'out onto water/upland' one. The scenario has three phases, a starting point in the common Athabaskan-Eyak system (position (1) on Map 6), as reconstructed by Leer;[44] then a movement of the system up the Chitina valley (a highly speculative stage), the way to the coast being blocked at the time by other, coastally adapted tribes; and, finally, a movement back to the coast down the Copper River in relatively recent times (ousted by the neighbouring Ahtna?), bringing the "Chitina valley" system with it. Notice on the map how the *niʔ/daʔ* axis shunts up the valley to stage (2) (where the Eyaks would have been 'upland' for the Ahtna), and, after a long period of isolation and internal change, reverses back to the Copper River valley to stage (3) (when the way was again free to the coast), becoming reformulated at some point as the modern Eyak *liʔ* vs. *dəG/ləG* opposition.[45] It will be seen that *daʔ* is now replaced by *ləG/dəG* 'upland, behind' since the meaning 'backwards, into a confined space' would still make sense for *niʔ* (now become *liʔ* in Eyak) as referring to 'downriver' as well as to entry into a confined space (as explained above in terms of the Copper River canyon), whereas the meaning of *daʔ*, 'in front, arriving at', no longer would make

44. Note that the double opposition of *yəX* vs. *dəG* and *cənʔ* vs. *nəG* has been collapsed for convenience – whereas the former pair were locally 'down' vs. 'up', the latter was used in a broader watershed sense 'downland (to the main river)' vs. 'upland (away from the main river)'. The two have become truly merged in Eyak, which seems to have become less river-oriented in phase (2), perhaps during its sojourn far up the Chitina valley and its smaller tributaries.

45. Perhaps at first just *liʔ* vs. *dəG*, with *ləG* remaining as 'up, upland'. Both are glossed as 'upland' by Krauss, but whereas *dəG* is used as a directional preverb in the sense 'upstream', *-ləG* is so only as the corresponding postposition, acc. Leer. In Krauss' dictionary (pp. 524f.) *ləG* is glossed as 'up from shore, ashore, up inlet, up river, to rear of house, behind'.

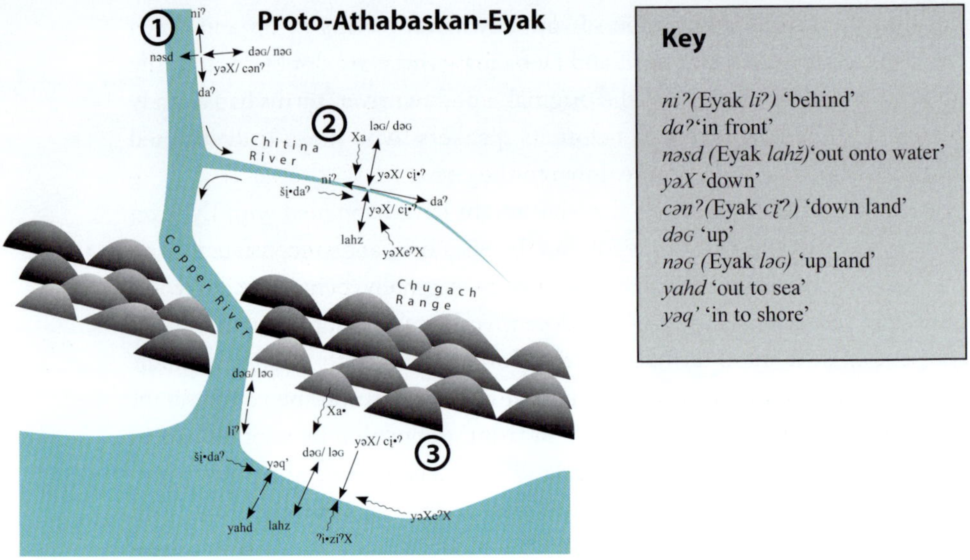

Map 6 Eyak.

sense for 'upriver'. It is possible that the original semantic opposition of 'in front' vs. 'behind' was still only loosely or secondarily applicable to rivers at this stage. All the other directions follow down to the coast as expected, including most of the wind terms. One important clue to all this is the wind direction yəXe?X, from the southeast, which would be etymologically understandable as (literally) coming 'down' (the meaning of yəX) to the Chitina River from the Chugach mountains (in fact it can still mean specifically 'down from the Chugach Range' according to Krauss' dictionary – but now towards the sea). Similarly with *šį·da?*, the westerly wind, which would literally have blown 'up the stream'.

The final result at stage (3) reveals the complete 'riverization' (or perhaps 're-riverization') of the system in a manner that still reflects in part its application along the Chitina (or other) *cul-de-sac*. The Proto-Athabaskan 'down to the water' vs. 'upland' axis now gains a coastal sense of 'out to sea (to the south)' vs. 'up from shore', and two new terms appear, *yahd* 'out to sea' (in any direction, perhaps the same as *yahd* 'out of') and *yəq'* 'in to shore'. One might further speculate that this third stage occurred prior to the appearance of the more expansive and aggressive (Eskimo) Alutiit from the west (somewhat less than a thousand years ago), which forced the Eyak further east along the coast into the highly marginal area of coast between the glaciers and the ocean as far as Yakutat, before the Tlingit appeared in that area from the southeast in recent centuries, pushing the remnant Eyak gradually back towards the west again. This particular scenario may not be the final word on the subject of the enigmatic origins of the Eyak of course, but at least it represents a coherent picture that accounts for the oddities of its orientation system.

One interesting matter specific to all the Na-Dene languages treated above which I shall not elaborate on here is the link between certain kinship terms and macrocosmic "watershed" terms applied to the interior of the house (see Leer, op. cit.: 101ff.). This apparently reflects traditional seating arrangements in the old style house, as for example in Koyukon when a man's primary wife traditionally sat towards the entrance (the river side) from her husband, and his secondary wife towards the back (away from the river).

6. Eskimo orientation revisited

Since writing my 1988 monograph on this subject more detailed information regarding directional terms for the Eskimo languages around Bering Strait and Bering Sea has come to light, and I have in consequence been able to get closer to answering the question posed there (and rather tentatively answered) as regards which came first, the riverine or the coastal version of the common Eskimo orientation system. This system is everywhere built up around a central opposition of the two demonstrative roots, *kiv-* (or *kiw-*) 'inside' and *ug-*'down there', which finds its ultimate justification in the nature of the traditional Eskimo house. There is a problem, however, with directly applying here the "orthogonality hypothesis" that I have proposed as a general diagnostic for systems that have moved from one geographical setting (e.g. inland) to another (e.g. the coast). This is because in coastal Eskimo (whether Inupiaq or Yupik) the microcosmic 'inside' vs. 'down' axis is usually orthogonal to its application to the coast, yet I have claimed that these systems are *originally* coastal and therefore should not display such orthogonal "skewing". Compare for example the directions given for Barrow (North Slope Alaskan Inupiaq – NAI) on Map 7.

A clue as to what is going on may in fact be found at Barrow, where the relationship is precisely *not* orthogonal: *kivan* (from *kiv-*) is the lefthand wall and *uan* (from *ug-*) the righthand one, which is parallel to the use of these roots along the coast, since the traditional house at Barrow faced away from the cold Arctic winds from the north (unlike most sites, where the entrance faced the water directly).[46] Further east (in eastern Canada) this axis is no longer applied within the house at all: although *ug-* (as in *uati*) still refers to the front wall, *kiv-* for the rear is replaced by independent locational nominal

46. The southern entrance was apparently also typical of the Mackenzie Delta and Copper Eskimo regions of the western Canadian Arctic. Interestingly, this situation is different at Point Hope, not far west from Barrow, where there are still traces of the *ug-* 'front wall' and *kiv-* 'back wall' opposition in place, namely in the forms *kivalliq* for the back room and *ualliq* for the front room of the house. This suggests that the Barrow development is a not particularly ancient innovation, one that brought the "macrocosmic" *ug-* vs. *kiv-* alignment back into the house, as it were, rather than projecting the microcosm onto the macrocosm.

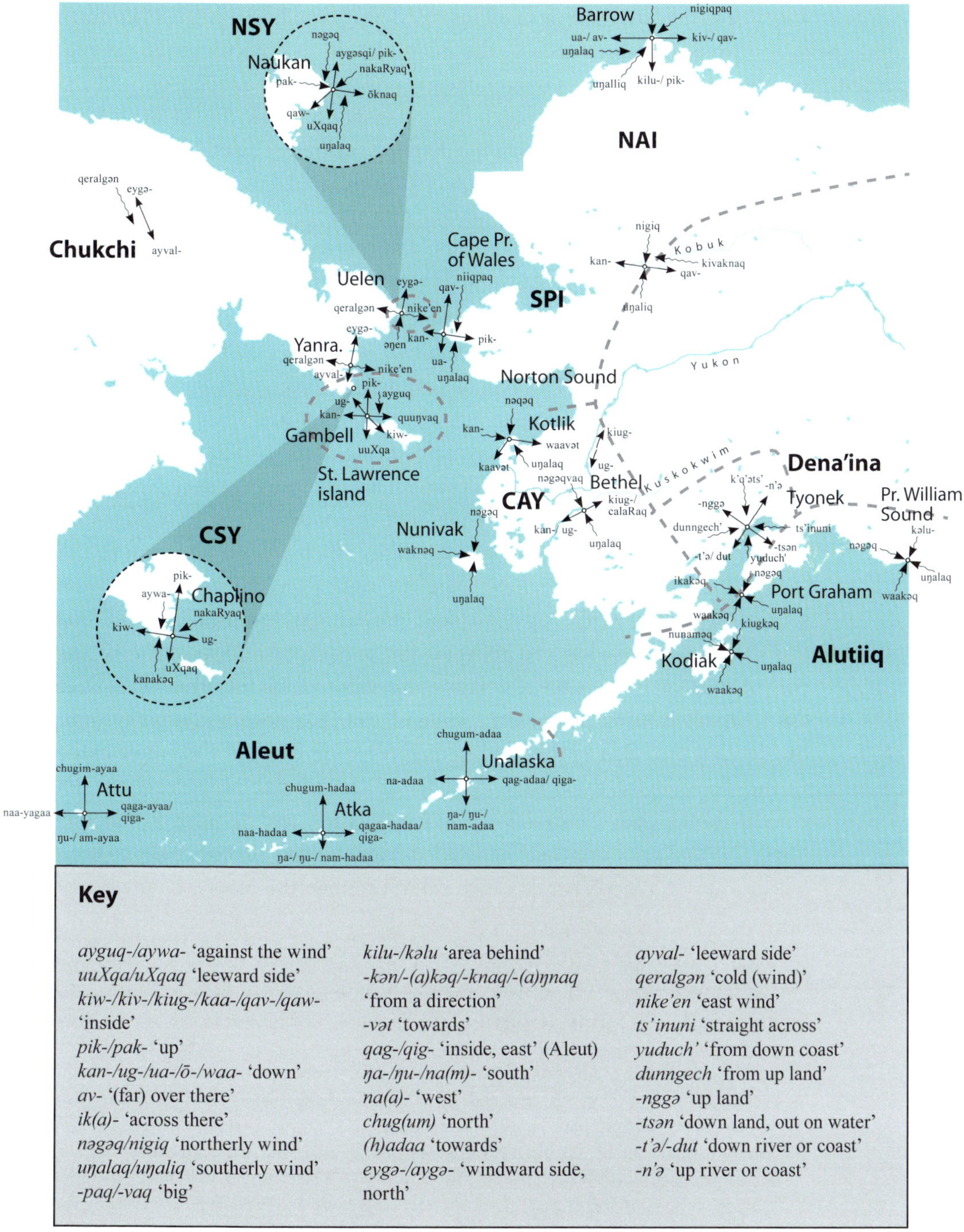

Key

ayguq-/aywa- 'against the wind'
uuXqa/uXqaq 'leeward side'
kiw-/kiv-/kiug-/kaa-/qav-/qaw- 'inside'
pik-/pak- 'up'
kan-/ug-/ua-/ō-/waa- 'down'
av- '(far) over there'
ik(a)- 'across there'
nəgəq/nigiq 'northerly wind'
uŋalaq/uŋaliq 'southerly wind'
-paq/-vaq 'big'

kilu-/kəlu 'area behind'
-kən/-(a)kəq/-knaq/-(a)ŋnaq 'from a direction'
-vət 'towards'
qag-/qig- 'inside, east' (Aleut)
ŋa-/ŋu-/na(m)- 'south'
na(a)- 'west'
chug(um) 'north'
(h)adaa 'towards'
eygə-/aygə- 'windward side, north'

ayval- 'leeward side'
qeralgən 'cold (wind)'
nike'en 'east wind'
ts'inuni 'straight across'
yuduch' 'from down coast'
dunngech 'from up land'
-nggə 'up land'
-tsən 'down land, out on water'
-t'ə/-dut 'down river or coast'
-n'ə 'up river or coast'

Map 7 Bering Strait/Bering Sea area.

kilu. In fact the latter is true of all Inuit dialects (including riverine Malimiut), so the riverine ambivalence of the microcosmic and macrocosmic orientation of the *ug-/kiv-* axis is obliterated everywhere.[47] It is actually only Siberian Yupik (which is clearly coastal) that presents a problem for the hypothesis as formulated, for here (at least in Chaplino) *ug-* refers to the front side (by the entrance) and *kiv-* the inner part of the house, just as in riverine Central Alaskan Yupik (CAY).

What is common to all the Yupik systems is the naturalness of using an 'in' demonstrative for the interior of the house and a 'down' one for the direction towards the water from the exit, given that the rich Eskimo demonstrative system is the main source of such expressions – see Table 1, from Jacobson (1984).[48] This will be orthogonal to the river banks or coasts in most locations (unlike at Barrow, where, as mentioned, the coastal sense appears to have "overruled" the microcosmic usage owing to the realignment of the house *vis-à-vis* the ocean). This idiosyncrasy may be specific to the Eskimo-Aleut language family and the nature of its demonstrative system. One might also argue that deciding which coastal direction to call 'down' and which 'in' ('left along coast' vs. 'right along coast') is at all events somewhat arbitrary (like 'up coast' and 'down coast' is in English), and that this can vary somewhat according to the geographical disposition of the convoluted Arctic coastline. Perhaps one needs to look for other clues as to the ultimate riverine or coastal source of the Eskimo orientation systems besides that provided by the "orthogonality hypothesis" – for example in the further breaking of the 'inside/outside' axis in the case of riverine but not coastal Yupik. Thus Central Siberian Yupik (CSY) and Naukanski Siberian Yupik (NSY) do not use their 'outside' demonstratives orthogonally to their 'inside' ones in macrocosmic usage any more than the coastal languages of

47. There are corresponding locational bases also in CAY, *kəlu-* 'away from river, back from house, behind' (not actually the rear part of the house in CAY, as in Inupiaq) and *kətə-* 'towards river, down in front, area away from wall (inside)'. The latter is 'south' in the King Island (SPI) variety of Inupiaq, and becomes 'west, towards the sea' in West Greenlandic. Another such word is *kaŋi(R)-* 'source, innermost part', which means 'back of house' in Alutiiq, 'indentation in shoreline' in CSY, 'source, place where peninsula joins mainland, headwater' in NAI, and ends up as 'east, land side, place where the smaller part of s.th. joins the larger part' in West Greenlandic.

48. The roots are found by removing the final *-na/-n'a* or *-vət* or *-ani* (the pronominal singular and adverbial allative and locative forms respectively). The category "extended" includes moving objects and "restricted" generally refers to a compact object, typically close by the speaker. The 'ug' digraph corresponds to /v/ in my citation of the root concerned (whereas 'ug' in *kiugna* corresponds to /g/ alone).

	Extended	Restricted	Obscured	
I a)	**man'a/maani**	**una/wani**	---	near speaker
b)	**tamana/tamaani**	**tauna/tuani**	---	near listener
II a)	**aûgna/avani**	**ingna/yaani**	**amna/amani**	over
b)	**agna/agaani**	**ikna, ikani**	**akemna/akmani**	across
III a)	**qaûgna/qavani**	**kiugna/kiani**	**qamna/qamani**	inside, upriver
b)	**qagna/qagaani**	**keggna/keggani**	**qakemna/qakmani**	outside
IV a)	**un'a/unani**	**kan'a/kanani**	**camna/camani**	down below, downslope
b)	**unegna/un'gani**	**ugna/uani**	**cakemna/cakmani**	downriver, toward exit
V a)	**paûgna/pavani**	**pingna/piani**	**pamna/pamani**	upslope
b)	**pagna/pagaani**	**pikna/pikani**	**pakemna/pakmani**	up above

Table 1 Eskimo demonstratives (Central Alaskan Yup'ik).

North Alaska do, but as riverine Central Alaskan Yupik does.[49] Note that I cite forms for NSY and CSY from the newer ANLC sources (Dobrieva et al. 2004 and Badten et al. 1987/2008 respectively).

There is however another, more positive factor that can help us here, one that is in line with what is known of pre-historical developments in the region, namely the possibility that the natural microcosmic 'down/in' axis of the Central Siberian Yupik coastal system was not originally employed (orthogonally) for directions along the coast of Bering Strait at all (*pace* Fortescue 1988). A closer look at the directions for CSY at Chaplino and Gambell on Map 7 suggests that this is still in large part so. The natural microcosmic axis ('in/down') extends homologously into the surrounding macrocosm (down to the shore), where it is orthogonally aligned to the *ayguq/uXqa(q)* 'north/south' prevailing wind one – the latter axis is areally stable throughout the Bering Strait/Bering Sea region and must have consisted originally of *nəgəq* vs. *uŋalaq,* as still on the Alaskan side. The shift to the 'wind side' vs. 'lee side' labels occurred later under Chukchi influence (I shall look more

49. Also Kobuk River Malimiut. In CAY the 'outside, out of door' demonstratives *qag-/qakm-* are at right angles to the direction given by the corresponding 'inside' roots (*kiv-/kiug-* and *qig-*) when referring to the macrocosm (but within the house they are, as expected, opposite to them). What ambiguity there is in the CSY system reflects more local variation. The situation at Gambell seems, for example, to represent in most respects a mirror-image of mainland Chaplino opposite (whence its population and language must at some point have come).

closely at this in the section on Eskimo-Chukchi interaction). Perhaps such a simple system was already in place by Punuk tradition times on St. Lawrence Island and the adjacent Chukotkan mainland, irrespective of whether the present Central Siberian Eskimos moved across from the Alaskan side or represent – at least in part – a survival from the Okvik tradition on the island.[50] The "bending" of the 'in/down' axis in Alaskan Eskimo to run parallel with the prevailing wind one could well have been a later development: witness the fact that the *ug-* direction is still today out to sea at both Chaplino and Gambell (respectively (south)east and (north)west) and its opposite, *kiw-*, points inland in a mirror-image relationship across the intervening strait.[51]

At Chaplino, note, a new 'north/south' axis has developed (replacing *nəgəq* vs. *uŋalaq*) that opposes restricted 'down to water' and 'upland' roots *kan-* and *pik-*, orthogonal to the *ug-/kiv-* axis (unlike in CAY, where these roots only have their immediate downland/upland-from-house senses – which is also the case in the North Alaskan coastal system). This is an areal Siberian Yupik phenomenon.[52] Naukanski Siberian Yupik of East Cape is more closely linked to the Alaskan side in this and other respects: it has maintained the 'north/south' *nəgəq/uŋalaq* opposition.

The development on the Alaskan side was probably different then, with riverine orientation developing at an early stage on the basis presumably of the Norton tradition (which lasted from ca. 500 BC to AD 200) as the latter became less and less coastally orientated. The inland CAY orientation of the house *vis-à-vis* the river can be seen in Figures 3 and 4, from Jacobson (1984)

50. Punuk developed out of the Okvik/Old Bering Strait "Neo-Eskimo" traditions (which appeared around Bering Strait about two thousand years ago) and lasted from ca. AD 800 to 1500. It influenced in turn the Thule tradition which was growing out of the Birnik phase in Alaska at about the same time. Note that the fragmentary directional data from Sirenikski (which may very well represent a residue from the earliest Neo-Eskimo presence on Chukotka) are paradoxical, with 'down' root *ug-* being glossed as 'northeast' (i.e. inland!) by Menovshchikov (1964). This only makes sense if it reflects the Chaplino sense of the root ('east'). The orthogonal use of *pik-* for north and *uqəX* (cf. Chaplino *uXqaq*) for south there, as also in Chaplino, supports this, and it is congruent with the fact that Sirenikski was heavily influenced lexically by CSY before becoming extinct.
51. Or generally further east along the island in the case of Gambell. Note that the removal in recent times of the Chaplino Eskimos to New Chaplino from Ungaziq out on the extreme southeastern tip of Chukotka would not have affected their basic orientation *vis-à-vis* St. Lawrence Island.
52. At Savoonga on St. Lawrence Island *pik-* may ambiguously refer to the local mountains (e.g. to the south of Savoonga) or to the mountains of Chukotka (roughly north, aligning with *ayguq*) – it also points north in Naukanski Siberian Yupik, aligning with *nəgəq*. At Gambell the "obscured" 'up' term *pam-* is used this way.

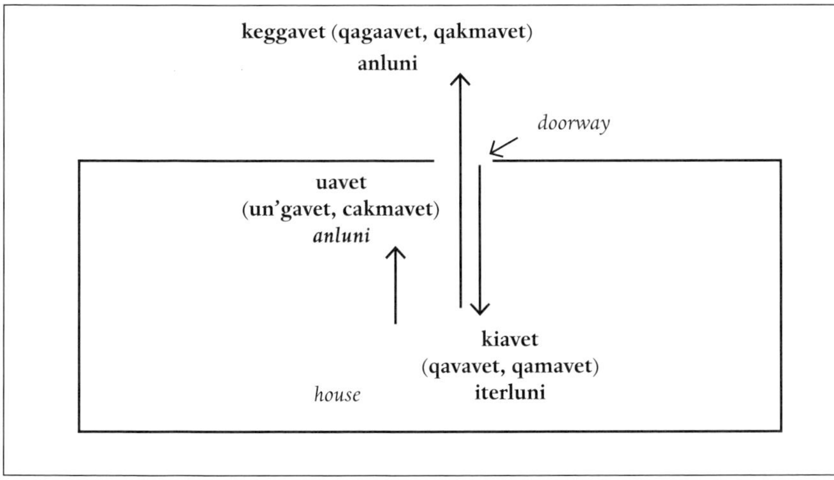

Fig. 3 Central Alaskan Yup'ik house-oriented directionals (Jacobson 1984).

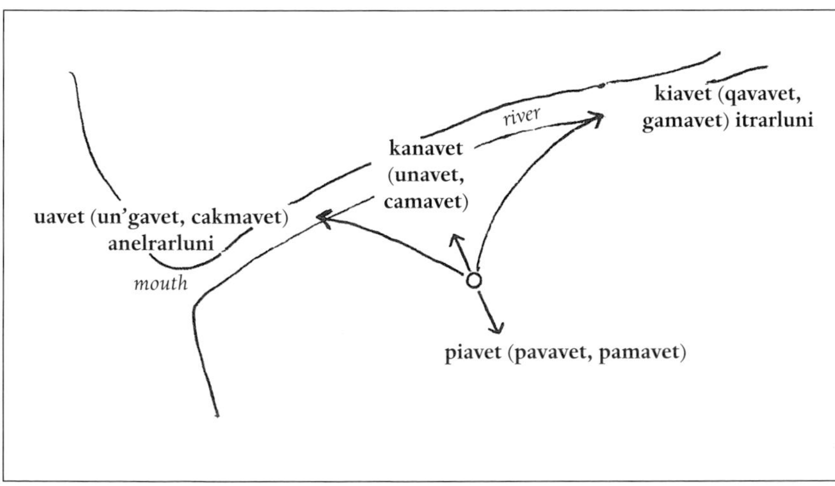

Fig. 4 Central Alaskan Yup'ik riverine directionals (Jacobson 1984).

– these contain all the relevant demonstrative roots (i.e. more than one 'in' and more than one 'down' root), but compare in particular the orientation of the *uavət* (<**ug-*) and *kiavət* (< **kiv-*) directions in the two figures. Coastal CAY, as around Norton Sound, is of particular interest since it would represent a later step back: a case of a riverine system coming down to the coast, maintaining the expected orthogonal ambiguity of the 'up/in' terms. At Kotlik (Walkie Charles, pers. comm.) the 'down' and 'in' directionals in *waavət* vs. *kaavət* (from **ug-* and **kiv-* respectively) refer to right and left along the coast, which seems a little illogical, but is consistent with the use of 'down' term *u(g)a-* (in *uassiaq*, a wind term) for 'west' at Golovin on the opposite side of the sound (wrongly marked at St. Michael in Fortescue 1988). This suggests that Kotlik speakers moved south around the bay from the south side of Seward Peninsula – note that the Norton Sound dialect is spoken on both sides of the sound although it is physically more or less split by the relatively late Malimiut Inupiaq incursion from the north (in the early 19th century). In other respects, Kotlik shares the same directionals as further inland on the Yukon river (e.g. with *nəgəq* 'north', *uŋalaq* 'south', *kiugnak* 'east', and *kanakliq* 'west'). As regards the "microcosm", *kaavət* is also 'towards the back of the house' at Kotlik, as expected of a riverine system.[53] The use of *ua-* on Nunivak Island for the opposite direction from that at Golovin and Kotlik may, on the other hand, represent a "mirror image" of the coastal directional axis on the mainland opposite (there appears to be an overlay of the riverine system of mainland Central Alaskan Yupik on an earlier coastal system on this large island, confusing the situation).

The sequence for the southwest Alaskan mainland (as only expressed rather indirectly on Map 1), would then have been (1) the adaptation of an ancient coastal system (on a Norton basis and shared at least in part by Aleut[54]) to the large rivers of southwest Alaska – hence the "orthogonal" relationship of the microcosmic and macrocosmic 'in/down' axis there; followed much later by (2), a return to the coasts of some CAY groups, notably on Norton Sound and Nunivak, reinforcing the orthogonal nature of the inland system, now brought back to the coasts.

A partially similar sequence may have occurred in northern Alaska with

53. NSY is more "Alaskan" than CSY also in this respect, displaying the same coastal opposition as in Norton Sound CAY of a 'down' term with an 'in' one referring to 'left along the coast' vs. 'right along the coast' respectively. Only it uses two different roots from the overall set, namely *sakm-* and *qaw-* (on St. Lawrence Island these refer to the west, towards Gambell, from Savoonga, and the reverse for *qaw-*, aligning with *ug-* and *kiv-*). As in Chaplino *ug-* refers rather to the east in NSY, out to sea (*uaknaq*), opposed to a 'back of house' term *kələvaaq* (< **kəlu*) referring to the west (inland). There thus appears to be a blend of the two systems in NSY.

54. Thus the Aleut 'south' term *ŋu-/ŋa-/na-* probably goes with *uŋalaq* of the same direction throughout Alaskan Eskimo, and its 'inside' direction *qig-* (corresponding to Eskimo *kiv-*) points back to the mainland to the east – as does 'outside' term *qag-*. The latter is the result, according to Bergsland (pers. comm.), of the entrance to the traditional house being to the east (through the roof), so both 'inside' and 'outside' lie in the same macrocosmic direction.

a Kobuk-like riverine system[55] (perhaps going back to the time of the still partially inland-oriented Ipiutaq culture of the area) brought back down to the coasts, only this time clashing with influence from (and contact with) CSY-speaking bearers of the coastal Punuk tradition in early Thule times. Whether or not they had already moved to the Siberian side or were still concentrated in the Seward Peninsula area at the time, these CSY speakers would still have had an "unambiguous" Norton-based coastal orientation system. This could have resulted in a kind of hybrid system. In other words, the application of the microcosmic 'in/down' opposition to waterways would have developed initially along the great rivers of Alaska, and when the Inupiaq-speaking Thule expansion brought northern Alaska into (renewed?) contact with the Asian side of the Bering Strait it would have resulted in a concomitant adjustment of the riverine system (already in place in most of Alaska, as still today in Kobuk River Malimiut) in order to facilitate communication with other coastal people around Bering Strait. The coastal application of the *ug-/kiv-* axis would have been a purely Alaskan phenomenon then. The original microcosmic sense of the opposition within the house (orthogonal to the macrocosmic one) would gradually have weakened as the Thule migrations moved further east (while Punuk groups, influenced in turn by Thule, moved southwest along the Asian coast), becoming more and more coastally focused. Finally it was replaced entirely, the 'along the coast' macrocosmic sense of the opposition having "won out", this being the essential orientational axis for all Inuit dialects today, from Alaska to Greenland. Although the etymological link to the 'in' and 'down' dimensions would persist it would no longer be transparent, and the axis would at all events no longer be in conflict with the reformulated microcosmic front wall vs. back wall opposition.

A variant of this scenario for North Alaska suggests itself: perhaps there was no direct influence from the Asian side during Punuk/Thule times and the Inupiaq coastal system was an independent development from a riverine Alaskan base. This would have involved both Inuit and Yupik coastal groups, presumably first around Seward Peninsula, the border area between the two, where today Seward Peninsula Inupiaq (SPI) is spoken, and would have included NSY before it moved over to fortress-like East Cape on the Asian side

55. New, supplementary forms for Malimiut have appeared since my 1988 monograph in Seiler (2005), who has *qaŋnaaq* 'towards northern coast (of Alaska)' (from *qag-* 'outside'), *kivaliRaq* 'east side, eastward', *nigiqpak* 'northerly wind, northwest', and (from *ug-*) *uatmun* 'southwest, towards Kotzebue from Noorvik' and *uaknaq* 'south or west wind'.

of the strait. In that case, the development of the North Alaskan coastal system was still more complex than I have suggested, the same in fact as for the coastal Yupik system (virtually identical with the Inuit one), i.e. from coastal origins (early Norton) to riverine (late Norton) and back to coastal (Thule).

7. Aleut: an archipelagoan system

As described in Fortescue (1988: 23ff.), the Aleut orientation system makes extensive use of the numerous demonstrative stems of that language, just like the related Eskimo systems. However, it is organized in a somewhat different fashion from both the coastal and the riverine Eskimo systems. The sense and orientation of the common proto-Eskimo-Aleut set of demonstrative roots has become adapted to the lay-out of the Aleut dwelling and its typical geographical setting, rocky volcanic islands devoid of rivers of any size. We appear to be dealing with a distinct "archipelagoan" variant, one without reference to river banks and also lacking the coastal relativity of the Inuit system with its "mirror-image" relationships across bodies of water (see the section on Nivkh concerning Kurile Ainu for a possible parallel).[56] This is not surprising, given the many small islands that make up this two thousand kilometre arc across the northern Pacific, since its cardinal points can hardly vary around the perimeter of every single island: there was constant travel back and forth along the chain, peaceful as well as war-like. The way of life is thoroughly maritime.

The orientation system itself is considerably simpler in its logic than the Eskimo ones, being more "absolute" as it follows an only slightly bending east-west axis crossed by a north-south axis shared by the entire chain, as can be seen on Map 7 (general Eastern Aleut terms on it are indicated at Unalaska). The system extends unchanged also to the Commander Islands (between Attu and Kamchatka) and to the Pribilof group north of Unalaska, to both of which Aleuts were moved in colonial times. Even though the Aleuts have been greatly shuffled around by forced movement at the hands of the Russian fur traders in the late 18th and early 19th centuries and by the

56. But note that the Kurile Islands are less of a *cul-de-sac* than the Aleutians – the northernmost Kurileans did move northward at some point to inhabit part of southernmost Kamchatka (they were there at the time of the arrival of the first Russians). The Aleutian Islands share with the Queen Charlotte Islands of British Columbia the feature of being a "residual zone" in Nichols's 1992 terms (this fits their situation better than the later term she prefers, "accretion zone", since there is no evidence of a "piling up" of successive languages on these isolated islands).

later events of World War Two, the system has everywhere remained intact, a sign of its remarkably long-term stability.

The specific point at which this system meshes with the Eskimo world is the eastern pole of its east/west axis, which correlates directly with the 'inward' direction of the Central Alaskan Yupik system on the mainland and the 'up coast' one of northern Alaskan Inupiaq, all of these being expressed by one or more common demonstrative roots meaning 'inwards' (in particular Aleut *qig-* < **qig*ʷ-, corresponding to Eskimo *kiv-/kiw-*). This makes sense when one observes the way the archipelago projects out from the Alaskan peninsula, which represents (especially along its north shore) the portal to the interior of the mainland at Bristol Bay. However, both the 'inside' (*qig-*) and the corresponding 'outside' demonstrative (*qag-*) are used of the east in Aleut. As mentioned in the previous section, Bergsland has pointed out that the orientation of the traditional Aleut house, with its roof entrance (by ladder) towards the east of the building, is probably the main factor here.[57]

The conflation of the macrocosmic directions of an 'outside' (*qag-*) and an 'inside' demonstrative in Aleut is from this point of view quite logical and it also explains the use of the stem originally meaning '(inside of) house' (*na-*) to mean 'west' in its orientation system (cf. *nag-* 'inside' and Eskimo *ənə* 'place, home'). Furthermore, most Aleutian villages are positioned along the northern sides of the islands – and this has a bearing on the term for 'north', which is based on stem *chug-*, probably cognate with *chuguX* 'beach' (Knut Bergsland, pers. comm.) and thus with Eskimo *ci(C)uRaq* 'sand'. The last of the four cardinal terms, that for 'south', variably *nu-, ŋu-, na-* or *ŋa-*, is in turn probably cognate with Eskimo *uŋalaq*, which is 'south' also in Central Alaskan Yupik (etymologically 'far over there', based on another, less productive demonstrative stem *uŋ(a)-* – cf. Fortescue 1988: 24). All four terms have cognates in Eskimo, then, and two of them have the same directional sense as there, aligning respectively with the Eskimo 'upstream/downstream' axis (coastal 'right/left along the coast') and the 'north/south' prevailing wind axis (down through the Bering Sea).[58]

57. Note that the word for 'doorway' in Aleut, *galRi-X,* is the same word as Eskimo *əgaləq* 'smokehole, window' (Bergsland 1986: 123).

58. Also *nəgəq*, the opposite to *uŋalaq* on the proto-Eskimo 'north/south' axis, has its reflex in Aleut according to Bergsland, namely *gi-* as in *gidgiX* 'breeze' – the fossilized suffix may have been a diminutive. Note that the Aleuts avoided directly naming the wind (especially a harsh one like *nəgəq*?) for fear of calling it up (cf. Jochelson 1966: 86), so the axis itself can perhaps be assigned to the proto-Eskimo-Aleut language.

Other demonstrative stems involved in the Aleut orientation system are *ag-* 'over there on the other side', *sað-* 'outside, towards the beach, to the seaside (of an islet)', *uð(aaRi)-* 'this side (of an islet)', *qak-* 'in there' (obliquely, e.g. down the entrance ladder, also 'at the bottom of a bay'), *aku-* 'over there to the side', and *iku-* 'there aside' (the last three are innovative "transversal" extensions of the proto-Eskimo-Aleut demonstratives, which may reflect the position of the entrance ladder within the Aleut house again). Virtually all additional terms for winds or intermediate directions are based on these directional roots, which are described in detail in Bergsland (1994, summarized on p. 568). It is noteworthy that the vertical 'down' vs. 'up' demonstrative roots, much used in Eskimo systems, are absent here. Actually this is logical if one thinks about it in an archipelagoan system: the 'up' demonstratives everywhere refer to up towards the centre of individual islands and thus can hardly refer to larger areas, although the root *haku-* 'up there aslant' has derived forms meaning 'up from the shore' everywhere (e.g. *(h)aku-uðaa* with *(h)uða-* 'direction'). A 'down' demonstrative is used for 'down on the beach' (*un(a)-*), which also forms *unaaGiX* 'outer, seaward' and *unaŋa-* 'passage between an island and land, shore side' (the source of the Aleut ethnonym *Unaŋan*, roughly 'seasiders' or 'beach dwellers'). All of these may be extended derivationally to form motion verbs.

Further items relevant to orientation, but not based on demonstrative roots, are *akinaX* 'leeward', *halim haðaa* 'windward', *tanaquu* 'land side' (based on *tana-*'land'), *(h)at-* 'outside, entrance (of a bay or house)' (and related *(h)achaRuu* 'open ocean' – otherwise *alaRuX*), and eastern *chaGat-*, Atkan *uðaga-* 'go out to sea, down to the seashore' (opposite of *(h)akuuGa-* 'come to shore', based on demonstrative root *haku-* above). There is also in fact a 'downstream' term, *atmuðuRan*, based on non-demonstrative positional stem *at-* 'down', but no corresponding 'upstream' term in Bergsland's compendious dictionary.

The Aleut data presented here casts some light on the question of which came first in Eskimo, the coastal or the riverine version of the common system, since the orthogonal relationship of an 'inwards' (*qig-/kiw-*) and a 'far over there' (*uŋa-*) demonstrative, as in Aleut, is reconstructible also for Proto-Eskimo. This, as I have argued, may reflect the source of both the riverine system of interior Alaska and the coastal system of the northern Alaskan and Chukotkan coasts and islands, perhaps dating back to early Norton times on the southwest Alaskan coast. The Aleuts may have started to move out onto the archipelago from the Alaskan peninsula as much as 3,500 years ago, not long after the first bearers of the Eskimo-Aleut language appeared on Seward Peninsula, but the typical Aleut house with the roof ladder entrance appeared on the archipelago only some 1,500 years ago (Dumond 1977: 67), i.e. after the Norton tradition (ca. 500 BC to AD 200) broke up in southwest Alaska. This would be compatible with the idea that the Aleut system is a reworking of the common Eskimo system prompted by a change of house type – as we shall see later, probably a house type that was there before their arrival in the region.

8. Chukotian systems: nomadic vs. sedentary

In the large area of Chukotka and Kamchatka, characterized by a number of distinct ecological settings and subsistence patterns, one finds considerable variation in the expression of geographical directions. Within Chukotka there are essentially just two types: a sedentary coastal system and an inland "nomadic" system, reflecting the distinction between "maritime" and "reindeer" Chukchis and Koryaks. As elsewhere in the Arctic and Sub-Arctic, the first kind of system is characterized by a combination of wind directions and coast-relative terms ('up/down the coast' and 'out to sea/upland'), while the inland "nomadic" system relies more on the passage of the sun and on the leeward/windward directions in relation to the prevailing cold wind out on the bare tundra. Neither of these rely much on 'upriver/downriver' terms, though these of course exist as independent items. This contrasts with the riverine system of the inland Kamchadals (Itelmen) of the lower half of Kamchatka which, as elsewhere in similar settings along major rivers, was oriented by river flow rather than by ocean and coast. I shall deal with this in a separate section on the neighbours of the Chukotians. None of this is unexpected given the respective environments in which the speakers of these languages live, yet there is much in the detail that is idiosyncratic, varying from location to location. In particular, there is the possibility of mixed varieties combining elements of the "pure" types, and of the reinterpretation of native directional terms as geographically "cardinal" through contact with the dominant national language of the region, namely Russian. These factors tend to confuse the picture, as they do elsewhere in the North Pacific region. Note that all of these variants are subsumed under what Levinson (2003: 90ff.) calls "absolute" spatial systems.

First, the "pure" coastal systems. I use the plural here since there appear to be various degrees of similarity to the typical Inuit coastal system described in Fortescue (1988). Also Siberian Yupik is of the coastal type, and, given the ethnohistory of the close interaction and inter-marriage between Chukchis and Eskimos on the Chukotkan peninsula in recent centuries, one must reckon with influence from Siberian Yupik on maritime Chukchi (and, less certainly, coastal Koryak and Kerek). This interaction will be examined more closely in the following section. The Chukchi have taken up sedentary residence on the coast of Chukotka more recently than the Eskimo population, whose language has been pushed to the extreme east of the peninsula. There nevertheless remain traces in coastal Chukchi that reflect the earlier inland orientation system preserved by reindeer Chukchis and Koryaks. For a description of the coastal system in its purest form one must refer to the works of Bogoraz (both the ethnographic description of 1904–9 and the dictionary of 1937). The information he provides is corroborated by still earlier sources – in particular Sarychev (1802). The essential dimension which establishes the parallel with the Eskimo coastal system is that of the opposing directions 'right along the coast' vs. 'left along the coast' (when looking out to sea), expressed by stems **ayval* 'leeward side' and **æygə* 'windward side' respectively.[59] The former may be related to *yaval(a)* 'behind' and the latter to *yəg-/igə-* 'blow (cold wind)'. This axis varies in absolute direction according to locality, just as in the Eskimo system. The same is true of a number of other important prevailing wind terms. This is less easy to see from more recent publications (in particular the Inenlikej school dictionary of 1982), which seem to reflect a standardization of cardinal 'north/south/east/west' terms throughout the area, no doubt reflecting Russian influence in the schools and elsewhere.[60]

The actual terms used in the original Chukchi coastal system as presented in Bogoraz (1904–9: 321–323) can be seen (in somewhat simplified form) on Map 8 for the Kolyma estuary and the mouth of the Anadyr River respectively; as for the third site he gives information for, the south side of Indian Point (near Chaplino at the southeast tip of the Chukotkan Peninsula), this has been combined on the map with the newer wind terms given for Yanrakynnot some way up the Bering Strait coast to the north of Chaplino supplied by Artur Apalu for the SIKU project (coordinated by Igor Krupnik of the

59. As with Eskimo, these are not expressed by the normal words for 'left hand' vs. 'right hand', i.e. *ŋacəŋ* and *mraŋ-* respectively (which, when extended by *-qac* 'side', can refer to extended directions to either side relative to the human body). Note that the reindeer Chukotians have special words for 'righthand draft reindeer' vs. 'lefthand draft reindeer' referring to the paired reindeers used for traction (in Chukchi respectively *gakaŋqor(a)* – i.e. 'harness reindeer' – vs. *ekvev*, probably related to *ekvet-* 'go away'). Terms referring to the left- vs. righthand side of the sledge (from the driver's perspective) are probably universal among people using sledges, whether drawn by dogs or by reindeer (certainly they are also found among the Tungusic herders).

60. In the school dictionary *qeralgən* has apparently become fixed as 'west', as opposed to *nike'en* 'east', with *aygəsqən* (from *eygə-*) as 'north' and *ayval(əsqən)* as 'south'.

Smithsonian Institution).[61] If you compare the absolute directions of the two opposing 'along-the-coast' terms as given by Bogoraz for Indian Point and the Kolyma estuary you can see that this axis swings around through approximately 90 degrees according to the way the coast faces. The corresponding directions marked on the map for Uelen and Chaun Bay (respectively from Inenlikej 1982 supplemented by Golbtseva from the SIKU project, and Zhukova & Kurebito 2004) seem to represent the more standardized "modern" directions as reflected in the school dictionaries and grammars (based on the (north)eastern dialect). In the Bogoraz dictionary of 1937 the form *aygəsqənqac* is given for 'north' (*-qac* is 'side, direction'), with no dialect indication, so this derived form might already have been "absolutized" earlier in that century. The detailed information given by Golbtseva best reflects the local Uelen terms today, with *eygəcqən* given as (geographical) 'north', and *eygənlik* as 'northwest' (lit. 'turning to the *eygə* direction).[62]

The forms for Uelen given by Golubtsova include the south wind *əŋen* (which I return to in the following section) and the north wind *gənoneŋ*, the latter related to *gənunnəkite* 'midnight' (also given as *gənunigən,* lit. 'centre wind', by Bogoraz for the Kolyma estuary). The new wind terms given for Yanrakynnot at the southeast end of the Chukchi peninsula can be compared to those for Uelen, where the coast is turned 90 degrees to the west. Whereas the east-west axis is the same at both localities, there are differences as regards the north-south one: Golbtseva gives *emnunigən* 'north' (lit. 'tundra wind' – note that the coast actually runs southwest/northeast here) and *ayvəsegən* 'south' (cf. *ayval* above and *igən* 'wind'). The latter use of stem *ayval* is as expected from Bogoraz, but its opposite, *eygəsqən* 'north' as at Uelen, is lacking (and Uelen in turn does not use *ayval* about the south). This situation, if correct, may reflect the greater stability of the east/west axis (as in

61. The only significant differences concern the exact directions of *qeralgən* and *nike'en* (southwest and northeast respectively at Indian Point acc. Bogoraz), which are still more or less opposite each other in both sources. Note that I keep Bogoraz' spelling of this term, which Inenlikej has as *nik'een* and Golbtseva as *nik'ejen* (the newer terms reflect regular phonological developments). There is also a discrepancy between the southwest wind given as *qaacgegən* in Bogoraz, which corresponds to *kaacge(g)ən* 'southeast wind' on Apalu's list (it is SSW in Uelen), probably 'wind along the edge of the hills/cliffs'. Bogoraz also has *eŋeneŋe* 'southeast wind', not given by Apalu, but compare the Uelen equivalent *əŋen* 'south wind' below.
62. The variation in vowels seen in related forms like this is due to vowel harmony, suffix *-qac* for instance requiring "dominant" /a/ instead of "recessive" /e/ throughout the word. The 'g' in Chukchi is a voiced velar fricative (as in Eskimo-Aleut) and the glottal stop is given by an apostrophe.

Map 8 Chukotko-Kamchatkan.

the original inland system) for Chukchi, as opposed to the north / south one – which in turn is more stable in neighbouring Eskimo.

The terms mentioned so far are all built up from native Chukotian stems and affixes, but a number of loans of directional words from or to Eskimo have been suggested in the literature. Although it is clear that there has been mutual influence in this area, it is not always easy to distinguish loans from calques, so I have singled this matter out for special treatment in the section that is to follow. One term that almost certainly is a loan from Eskimo is *nike'en*, a major wind from off the sea in most places, which can also be seen to vary according to locality on the map – it is reported, for example, as 'east' at Yanrakynnot and Uelen, but as 'northeast' at Indian Point and the Anadyr estuary, and as 'northwest' at the Kolyma estuary by Bogoraz. This term corresponds to Eskimo *nakaRyaq*, a northeast wind in Siberian Yupik (with the same stem possibly found in Kodiak Island Alutiiq *nakiRsaRiiq*). The phonological correspondences are paralleled in other borrowings going either way (cf. de Reuse 1994: 341). The plausible Eskimo etymology ('descending wind') and lack of a Chukotian one tips the balance in the direction of this being an Eskimo loan into coastal Chukotian.

The varying directions of the cold inland wind *qeralgən* on the map I shall return to below in connection with the inland system, from which it has probably been carried over. Note also the various wind directions involving the stem **æmnuŋ* 'tundra' (also in Kerek, where *amnuŋ* is just 'north'), which can be compared to the 'up' direction term for inland in the coastal Eskimo system, in so far as the tundra is situated above the cliffs that surround most of the Chukotkan peninsula.

Moving down the coast from the Chukchi to the Kerek and coastal Koryak, most of the terms used here are familiar from further north, including the wind term *əŋen/əŋinnə*, everywhere a warm wind and usually from the east, but, as mentioned, found in the sense 'south' at Uelen.[63] However, the 'south' term of the coast direction pair is replaced beyond Kerek (i.e. in Koryak) with others referring to 'down' (e.g. with stem *iwtə-*), i.e. 'down towards the Kamchatkan isthmus' if not just 'down from the tundra'. Already in Bogoraz' wind rose for the mouth of the Anadyr we note the lack of the 'left / right along the coast' terms for north and south (replaced by *qitənike'en*,

63. Bogoraz has *eŋeneŋe* 'southeast wind' for Kamenski Koryak at the head of Penzhina Bay. He also has *empeikin* 'northeast wind', *qeyalgən* 'west wind' and *ewtelan* 'south(west) wind' for there.

lit. 'cold *nike'en*' and *yagnaigən* 'counter/meeting wind' respectively). It is not at all clear whether the individual Bogoraz received these from could be considered a "maritime" Chukchi at all – this flat, inland-oriented area is at all events not original coastal Chukchi territory. In fact, Bogoraz specifically referred to the Chukchi group north of the Anadyr (as far as Holy Cross Bay) as "reindeer Chukchi". In the 17th century the Anadyr basin was actually inhabited by Yukagirs. Kerek, on the other hand, like coastal Koryak (i.e. the coastal dialects such as the Kamenski, plus the separate language Alutor), is clearly oriented towards the sea.[64] The data available for Kerek is, however, not very reliable, since the last speakers of the language, from whom Asinovsky elicited his unpublished data (incorporated in Fortescue 2005), were much influenced by Chukchi. Bogoraz has *attaRə(y)ol* 'downriver, down coast' (lit. 'in front') in his Kamenski Koryak texts, a clear indication of the coastal nature of this dialect.

In coastal Koryak *eygə* is used for the northern direction like on the Chukotkan peninsula – although here it is everywhere fixed to mean more or less cardinal north and does not swing around as radically as the equivalent in the "pure" coastal Eskimo system (in Alutor *eygəsqən* can still mean both 'north' and literally 'against the wind'). It is unclear whether this is due to standardization again (Bogoraz did not give this term for Kamenski, unfortunately), or whether it merely reflects a less developed coastal system, one less influenced by distant Eskimo neighbours. There is at least a certain relativity of directional terms between the parallel east and west coasts of the Kamchatkan isthmus, i.e. the difference between the sense of *vəligəŋ*, an onshore wind, in the Pacific dialect (Alutor proper) and the Okhotsk sea (Palanski) dialect: as expected these are respectively an east and a west wind.[65] Note that the Koryak reflected in the wind rose on Map 8 (for the vicinity of Ewensk, from Zhukova & Kurebito 2004) is not "maritime", though the speakers are now sedentary, living not far inland, and apparently no longer herd reindeer on the tundra (whether this is now true also of the nomadic Koryaks who moved to the interior of Kamchatka is not clear). This sys-

64. Actually the Alutor were traditionally only semi-sedentary, combining fishing, sea-mammal-hunting and reindeer breeding (Levin & Potapov 1956: 854–855). The dwellings of the maritime Koryak faced towards the sea, while the *yaranga* of the inland herders faced the sunrise, like that of the inland Chukchi (Jochelson 1908: 456).

65. There is also some variation of wind directions within quite restricted areas of coast, as for instance in the case of *iwiniŋ* 'blow a west wind' at Vyvenka but 'blow a north wind' at Anapka, both on the east coast (cf. *iwini-* 'go out to sea').

tem seems to combine original sun-oriented inland terms for east and west (see below) with coastal ones for north and south. M. Kurebito (2001 and pers. comm.) has several alternative terms for 'south', including *omnotaŋqal* (lit. 'warm land direction'), *yoyoRəŋqal* (lit. 'stormy direction') and *ewtəlaŋqal* ('down below'), and from an inland reindeer herding brigade: *aygəvacəŋqal* 'south' (vs. *aygətqəŋval* 'north') – this may be a blend with (or reanalysis of) an original **ayvacəŋqal* (cf. the stem in Kerek *aywanaŋa* of this meaning – it has disappeared entirely from Koryak and Alutor). For Alutor she also has *ŋəpegən* (from *ŋəp-* 'get down') in this meaning. This suggests recent sedenterization on or near the coast subsequent to loss of the second term of the *eygə* / *ayval* axis, although the 'down' terms look suspiciously like having an original coastal origin in so far as south is literally down from inland in this region.[66]

Let us return now to the inland orientation system of the nomadic "reindeer" Chukchi, who traditionally moved with their herds from the borders of the Kolyma taiga to the west as far as the interior of the Chukotkan peninsula to the east, with what appears to have been a very uniform language and culture. We have to rely largely on Bogoraz (1904–9) for our information, although luckily his account of the system – including its relation to the interior of the *yaranga* (the traditional tent) – is quite detailed. Here we find the original orientation of the *eygə* vs. *ayval* opposition, namely from northwest to southeast, the northwest being the source of the coldest winds blowing across the Chukotkan high tundra. The western nomads call the eastern ones *ayval'ət* and the eastern ones called them in turn *eygəsqəl'ət*, based on these stems. They also correlated (as in the inset to Map 8) directly with the way in which the *yaranga* was set up, with the entrance towards the northeast, the direction of the dawn, and the righthand wall of the interior sleeping compartment (seen from the tent entrance) consequently facing the northwest (*aygəsqə-ron*), while the opposite, lefthand wall faced southeast (*ayval-lon*).[67] Now the northeast orientation of the entrance of the *yaranga* was of ritual as well as physical significance: it faced the direction of *təŋa(g)*

66. Why 'south' terms should be in general more variable in the Chukotian region than are 'north' ones is an interesting but open question (with parallels elsewhere). Perhaps it reflects a conflict between the interior and coastal relevance of this direction in the vicinity of the Koryak "homeland".

67. This is different on the coast at Uelen, acc. Golbtseva, where the entrance to the *yaranga* was apparently facing west (probably northwest up along the coast – the southeast wind is colloquially called *kətləganlejpə təlig'i* 'blowing from the back of the *yaranga*').

ərgən, the Morning Dawn, the most important of these ritual directions (after the zenith) for sacrificing to the spirits. The directions themselves were regarded as animate spirits according to Bogoraz (op. cit.: 303f.). A number of other sun-related directional terms from this ritual set are found in use among the nomadic Chukotians, notably those for 'sun up' and 'sun down', even though these would change significantly in their absolute geographical senses according to the season of the year. The latter must be kept close track of by nomads of the far north as they move their herds around in predetermined cycles.

The most complete wind rose for such terms (apart from Bogoraz' array of ritual directional "spirits") is that recorded by Sarychev (1802) in connection with the Billings expedition. He recorded *tirkətətvə* for 'west' (lit. 'sundown'), *tirkinini* 'east' (lit. 'sunrise'), and *tirkipadga* 'south' – corresponding to reindeer Koryak *tikipata* (the first part of the latter is 'sun').[68] He also had *keralgən* (for *qeralgən*) 'north', literally 'cold (wind)'. This term is still used in this sense today in the far western inland part of the Chukchi territory at Bilibino according to Golbtseva. Elsewhere, on the coasts, it refers variously to the direction towards the coldest prevailing local wind, thus at the Kolyma estuary towards the south, but at Uelen towards the west. It is 'northwest' in "reindeer" Koryak (where, as noted, one also finds the 'sundown' and 'sunrise' terms for 'west' and 'east').

This all makes sense when considering the life style of inland nomads, and it is indeed a pattern found with other nomadic groups of the Russian Far East, such as the Evens and Evenkis (otherwise known as Lamuts and Evenks respectively), where east and west are similarly referred to as sunrise and sundown respectively. The 'south' term in these Tungusic dialects is generally expressed by some word referring to warmth (of the sun). In Koryak (all varieties) there are, as we have seen, alternative terms for 'south' based on a stem meaning 'warm' (*om-*), just as in neighbouring Even. Although these groups may cross large rivers, they do not follow them as major orientation parameters. All varieties of Chukotian (northern Chukotko-Kamchatkan) share 'upriver/downriver' terms, as in Chukchi *gərgoca* 'on top, upriver' (Alutor *gərgus(aŋ)*), and Koryak *ewcə(caŋ)* 'downriver' (cf. Chukchi *ewəca* 'below, under'), but these are largely independent of other directional

68. The second part is uncertain but either reflects *əp-* 'stick in, attach', parallel to the Chukchi name of the Pole Star *unp-eŋer* (i.e. the 'attached star'), or cognate with Chukchi *terkəpgat-* 'go up (sun)'.

terms and do not form part of the primary orientation system (*ewəc-* is probably related to the 'down' root *iwtəl-* found in the sense 'south' in Koryak however).

In fact, there is reason to believe that the inland Chukotians as a whole may have gone from being coastally oriented directly to adaptation to an interior, nomadic way of life without passing through a riverine phase. They all seem to derive (linguistically at least) from the Old Koryak culture which, starting some 2,000 years ago, eventually stretched from the vicinity of modern Magadan as far as the mouth of the Anadyr and down the coast of western Kamchatka.[69] This in turn developed from the still earlier Tokareva culture of the Okhotsk coast according to archaeologists like Lebedintsev (1998). It is possible, however, that the Chukchi split off from the Tokareva phase before the development of Old Koryak. The "dual subsistence" model of Krupnik (1993) suggests a cyclical shift in Siberia between coastal adaptation (during warmer periods) and the return to interior subsistence patterns (during colder periods). There was in fact a colder period in the centuries prior to the emergence of the Old Koryak culture, which was formed during a warmer period (see Petersen & Rex 1982 for the swings in high latitude temperatures reflected in Greenland ice core samples). Much later, during the "Little Ice Age" around the 15th century, conditions would again have been conducive to a return inland, this time resulting in a major shift in subsistence pattern as seems to have occurred around the 13th to 16th century, when large-scale reindeerherding developed in the tundra environment (cf. Fortescue 1998: 192).[70] Alutor (and other purely "maritime" forms of Koryak) may in other words never have gone through an inland reindeer-herding phase such as the coastal Chukchis did – in fact this language does not show any obvious sign of the anomalies suggestive of a major shift of environment we have seen elsewhere. An adjustment to Map 1 in this area might thus be required.

To find a true riverine system in the Chukotko-Kamchatkan area we need to move further south to the distantly related southern division of the fam-

69. Of course nothing precludes a still earlier interior origin of at least some of the people behind the Old Koryak Culture (and related groups further north), when the hunting of wild reindeer may have been the principal form of subsistence before adaptation to the coast. At this time depth ethnic and linguistic identity begin to unravel, however.

70. It is believed that it was through contact with Tungusic herders (perhaps starting as early as the 8th or 9th century) that the Koryaks and then the Chukchi learnt reindeer-husbandry as such, although the Evens and Evenkis themselves mainly used their domestic reindeer for transport and for decoying wild reindeer rather than developing large-scale herding.

ily, namely that of the sedentary Itelmen of the southern half of Kamchatka (once extending further north towards the isthmus), who have more in common with the riverine fishermen of the Amur River than with the Chukotian nomads.

9. Eskimo-Chukchi interaction at Bering Strait

It is relatively rare among the North Pacific Rim languages for the orientation systems of two different groups that come into close proximity with one another to mutually adjust or for one to accommodate to the other – as opposed to the common situation where a system adjusts in a predictable way to new geographical circumstances. At least, it is difficult to distinguish the two possibilities on purely linguistic grounds. However, there is one clear-cut case where this has indeed happened, namely on the coasts of the Chukotkan peninsula, where Chukchis and Eskimos have interacted and intermarried for centuries. The cultural and subsistence pattern effects of this meeting are well documented, most of them being explicable in terms of the originally nomadic reindeer-herding Chukchis adapting to the maritime way of life of the Eskimos who were already on the coasts when they started moving down from the open tundra to stay rather than just trade. The effect of this (protracted) event on the original orientation system of the Chukchis has not been investigated until now. The result was predominantly one-way, the only obvious lexical loan from Chukchi to Eskimo being a word for 'north' (*eygəsqə*), originally 'windward side' – I shall return below to the coincidental similarity of this word to a native Eskimo word *ayguR-* 'go against the wind', which played a role in this apparent "borrowing".

How does the adjustment of an original inland, nomadic orientation system to coastal life of the Eskimo kind manifest itself – and how can one be so sure that this is just what happened? Luckily the original inland system (still in use among reindeer-herding Chukchi and Koryak groups) has been well described by Bogoraz (1904–9 and 1937), and good contemporary data is available for various coastal sites today (as selectively shown on Map 8). The latter system is more variable according to location than is the former, being relative to the coast-line in a manner similar to the coast-relative systems of Inupiaq and of Siberian Yupik. As we have seen, however, standardization under the influence of the colonizing language (in this case Russian rather than English) has reduced this variability since Bogoraz's time.

Let me start by repeating what was said in the previous section as regards the inland system described by Bogoraz (essentially the same everywhere).

It consisted of the windward vs. the leeward directions (*eygə* vs. *ayval*) *vis-à-vis* the prevailing (cold) wind across the high tundra. This varied somewhat from area to area but was quintessentially from the northwest, and was supplemented by 'sunset' vs. 'sunrise' terms, which again could vary, but this time in a universal manner according to season. The inland Chukchi clearly paid great attention to the precession of these solar positions and indeed personified them as directional "spirits", as we have seen. Only midday and midnight lay in a fixed direction. There are other specific wind terms, in particular the cold wind *qeralgən* (literally 'cold'), which varies in absolute direction, aligning either with the prevailing northwest wind (as mentioned above) or diverging from it, coming from further westward or further northward according to locality.

Now it is important to realize that this inland (non-riverine) system was brought down to the coast in several distinct places and the ensuing adjustments were somewhat different according (in particular) as to whether there was a concentration of sedentary Eskimos already there or not. This was not the case at the estuaries of the Anadyr and Kolyma rivers (flowing into the Bering Sea and the Arctic Ocean respectively): these were not sedentary Eskimo areas – nor was it the case in the area where the nomadic Koryaks (with a similar inland system) came down to the coast at the Kamchatkan isthmus.[71] What appears to have happened in all these cases is that the *eygə/ayval* axis became linked to orientation along the coast rather than to the prevailing inland wind, with *qeralgən* still generally coming from the northwest direction however (refer back to Map 8 again). Moreover, a new wind term, *nike'en*, appears – generally a milder wind coming from off the sea. The latter may in fact indicate an early Eskimo presence on the coast at some of these far-flung localities, since the word appears to be Eskimo in origin, as we have seen earlier.

As far as I can tell, however, these adaptations of the original inland system to the coast never developed in these areas into a "pure" coastal system of the Eskimo type in which there are dedicated 'up/down coast' words that vary continuously in absolute orientation as the coast meanders in various directions (everywhere 'left' vs. 'right' along the coast as you look out to sea).

71. The coastal system of the Kerek appears to have been much like that of the neighbouring Chukchi of the Anadyr estuary, by whom their language was, as mentioned, rather strongly influenced and with whom they intermarried before the language (recently) became extinct. The Kamenski word meaning both 'downriver' and 'down coast' mentioned in the perevious section is idiosyncratic and is not related to the realignment of the 'leeward/windward' terms in coastal Chukchi.

This is the essential difference that appears in the contiguous area around the Chukotkan peninsula where Chukchis coming down from the tundra to the coast did indeed meet a sedentary Eskimo population already in place. Bogoraz made a point of stressing the relativity of the *eygə/ayval* axis according to the direction the coast faced in different localities around the peninsula (towards the Arctic Ocean or the Bering Sea/Pacific Ocean). This is not the case at the Kamchatkan peninsula, for example, if one compares the east and west coasts of the isthmus, where the *eygə* direction is north on both sides of the isthmus (in Alutor proper and Palanski respectively).

This contrasts with the situation on the Asian side of Bering Strait. Here the terms *ayval* 'south' around Bering Strait (in Bogoraz 'right along the coast') and *ayvan(a)* 'Eskimo' have become entangled. As we have seen, the first Chukchi word here meant originally 'leeward side' as opposed to *eygə* 'windward side', which, it has been suggested in the literature (e.g. by de Reuse 1994: 410, citing Vdovin), may have given Central Siberian Yupik (CSY) *ayguq*, *aywa-* 'north'. However, there is a good Eskimo source for the latter, namely *ayguR-*, proto-Eskimo **aðguR-* 'go against the wind or current', so this is probably indicative of a coincidence. The Chukchi word for Eskimo, *ayvan(a),* may indeed come from the CSY, but must at least have been influenced in meaning by the native Chukchi word (recall that the western Chukchi call the easterners *ayval'ət*). To complicate the situation, neighbouring Naukanski and Sirenikski Eskimo have directly borrowed Chukchi *aygəsqən* in the sense 'north', *aygəsqə* and *aygəsqəX* respectively, and all Siberian Yupik uses the native word *uXqaq* 'south, leeside' as the opposite of *aygəsqə(n)* 'north, windside', so the whole north/south axis appears to have been taken over from Chukchi by Siberian Eskimo – conceptually at least (for further details see Fortescue 2005: 18, 27).

What appears to have happened around the Chukotkan peninsula, then, is that the original *eygə/ayval* axis has become associated with the parallel Eskimo *nəgəq/uŋalaq* one running north/south through Bering Strait, which opposes a cold northern wind with a milder southern one (refer back to Map 7). Now this axis is somewhat more "absolute" around the Bering Strait and adjacent Bering Sea area than the 'down/up coast' terms based on the multifarious Eskimo demonstrative roots (lacking in Chukotian) – the *nəgəq/uŋalaq* axis only begins to swivel, so to speak, further east, reflecting the Thule migrations in that direction, and something similar is true of the parallel *eygə/ayval* amongst the coastal Chukchi as it swings to the west. In general, the coastal Chukchi system is not quite as "coast-relative" as the

Eskimo coastal system as a whole, although Bogoraz's testimony makes it clear that there was at least a coast-relative shift in orientation between the Arctic and Bering Sea coasts of the peninsula, as indeed in the orientation of the *nike'en* wind, which also shifts in a more or less predictable manner as one follows the coast. I have mentioned that the latter term is probably borrowed from the Eskimo, and this may be true also of another purely coastal wind term we have come across in Chukchi, namely *əŋen* ('south' at Uelen), which is also found in Alutor (where it is an "unhealthy" east wind). It is unetymologizeable in Chukotian, but could reflect Eskimo *uŋalaq*, also used of 'south' down Bering Strait.[72] This is an ancient Eskimo term, also reflected in all likelihood in Aleut *ŋa-/ŋu-/na-* 'south', as discussed earlier. As a *curiosum,* note that this wind and its opposite at the Kolyma estuary, the icy *qeralgən*, are anthropomorphized as respectively a woman and a man, drawn towards each other but always quarreling as they pass (Bogoraz 1904–9: 323). This is reminiscent of the similar conceptualization amongst the Inuit of Igloolik described by MacDonald (1998: 175f.), where the northwest wind *uangnaq* is the fickle female wind, and southeast *nigiq* the more steady male one.

Let us return to the question of the "coincidental" formal similarity of the 'north' terms in coastal Chukchi and Siberian Yupik (all varieties). This was discussed briefly in Fortescue (1988). As mentioned there, it has been suggested in the past that we are dealing here simply with a loan from Chukchi to Siberian Yupik, but I do not believe that explanation can be the whole story. It seems more likely that Siberian Yupik has been influenced only conceptually by Chukchi, opposing as it does a north term, *ayguq*, from a base meaning 'go against the current or wind', to a south term, *uXqaq*, literally 'lee side', parallel to Chukotian *aygə* vs. *ayval*. Now *eygə* can also be used verbally of going against the wind, just as CSY *ayguR-*, of which *ayguq* is a nominalized form. This formal coincidence (if it does not reflect a very ancient cognate) would have furthered the adaptation of the native term for the cardinal direction – something that has not happened in other varieties of Eskimo sharing it. In the other two varieties of Siberian Eskimo, Naukanski and (now extinct) Sirenikski, where the contact with Chukchi was stronger than on Saint Lawrence Island, the Chukchi word for 'north' itself, in the form *aygəsqə,* has simply been borrowed as such.

72. Note that Chukchi loans from Eskimo words ending in /q/ usually end in /n/, a singulative marker much like the former. However, the loan may reflect the nominalized form of the root, *uŋan*, which in Eskimo languages has the specialized meaning 'area beyond', and in Seward Peninsula Inupiaq means 'south'.

So the adjustment of the two systems has been to some degree mutual, with the Eskimo input to the resultant "blend" being somewhat stronger than the Chukchi – which is not surprising given that it was the Chukchi who, although they played the more aggressive role in pushing the Eskimo languages back towards their present enclaves, adapted to the Eskimo way of life on the coast, and not the reverse. All the directional and wind terms of Saint Lawrence Island CSY are thus probably of purely Eskimo origin – and this includes all the 'east/west' terms (and some alternative 'north/south' ones), which are based on the pan-Eskimo demonstrative roots.

10. Nomadic and riverine neighbours of the Chukotians

There is, unfortunately, only very sporadic information about the original three varieties of "Kamchadal" (as southern Chukotko-Kamchatkan was previously called). That for which there is the best information, western Itelmen, the only surviving language, has been strongly influenced by neighbouring Alutor ("maritime Koryak"), but even so it is clear that we are dealing with a riverine system, probably much like that in the Kamchatka River valley which constituted the main geographical axis of the eastern Itelmen. The western Itelmen of Khajruzovo, Kovran and Sedanka, like their fellow Kamchatkans further east and south, who have for over a century spoken only Russian, live for the most part well inland along the salmon-rich rivers of this large peninsula. The two main dialects – northern at Khajruzovo and Kovran, southern at Sedanka – appear combined on Map 8 owing to the limited data available for wind directions in either. Although one can construct a wind rose much like that for Koryak from entries in dictionaries and word lists such as Volodin & Xalojmova (1989) and Zhukova & Kurebito (2004), most of the relevant terms are either borrowed from or glossed on the corresponding Koryak and/or Russian. Thus *ayvaŋ* 'north' – Sedanka *eyen* – is from Koryak *aygə*, and *tnŭm* 'south' is literally 'down' like Koryak *iwtəl-*, while *eymen* 'west' (Sedanka only) is probably from Alutor *yamigən*, 'north' at Vyvenka but 'west' at Anapka, which, according to Bogoraz, has a Chukchi cognate at the Kolyma estuary (*yamwajgən*, probably from *yaŋvə-* 'bay') and also a Kamenski (Penzhina Bay) Koryak one (*empeikin* 'northeast'), all containing *igən* 'wind'. The only word attested for 'east' is Russian *vosxod*. The older system would appear to have been sun-related – at least as regards north and south – as reflected in Radlinski (1891–4, collected by the exiled Pole, Benedikt Dybowski). He has *kinnyn kink* (lit. 'midnight') for 'north' (but also *emigin*) and *kinnyn klchil* (lit. 'midday') for 'south' for western Itelmen. For 'west' he has *yameyinkamen*, undoubtedly going with the Alutor form above.

As is made clear in Xalojmova et al. (1996), however, 'upriver' vs. 'downriver' (respectively *xan'c-* vs. *eyan-*) is the essential dimension for orientation among the Itelmen. This is supplemented by further terms *sen(ke)* 'in(to) the forest' (on either side of the river), and *salaŋ(ke)* 'across (to) the other side'. There are also special verbs for going upriver and downriver (as well as the usual relative terms 'in front of', 'behind', 'to the left' and 'to the right').[73]

It is difficult to make much of the older terms recorded for the two other major varieties of Kamchadal – the accuracy of the few forms recorded for the extinct southern and eastern varieties leave much to be desired, though Krašeninnikov does have *eemyxt* 'west wind' for the eastern language (which may be comparable to western *eymen* 'west' above), but also *bykymyg* at Kamchatka River, which seems to go rather with *makman* 'northwest wind' in the southern language and perhaps *mokavrač* 'strong wind' in the western language (the last two from Radlinski). Radlinski has *kysk* 'east' for the eastern language, cross-referencing it from *kleċ inuneziċ* 'sunrise' (lit. 'sun growing', as opposed to *kleċ iċksiċ* 'sunset') – if there is a true etymological link this suggests a thoroughly sun-based system for older Itelmen (compare eastern *knukolič* 'midday' and *knuchuguig* 'midnight' with the old western forms above). A complete wind rose was recorded for the southern language by Dybowski (i.e. in Radlinski 1891–2), and one can guess at the etymological source of some of these terms. Radlinski gives for example a southeast wind term for the southern language (*kiniulp*) that may be related to 'midday' (compare *kinnyn klchil* in the western language above),[74] and an east wind term (*acvaspil*) that could be related to Chukotian *ayval* 'lee' (the latter part contains *spil* 'wind', as also in *katispil* 'southwest wind' – cf. *katikich* 'go past'). There is a prefix *vi-* (from **lvi-* 'real'?) in a couple of derived forms, *viacvastil* 'northeast wind' (for *vi-acvaspil*?) and *vimakman* 'north wind' (from *makman* above). The term for 'west' (also used of that wind), *tezis*, could go with (*kaač*) *tuut skiskik* '(the sun) goes down'. Anything beyond this is pure speculation – many of Radlinski's forms are badly distorted.

Moving from the south to the west of the Chukotians, we meet a completely different language family, Tungusic (traditionally regarded as a branch of "Altaic"), which moved down to the coast from the upper Amur and Baykal regions at a relatively late date, with northern reindeer-herding

73. The 'left' and 'right' terms (*sic'eŋ-* vs. *xtoŋ-* respectively) can, like in Chukotian, be used of directions extended out from a human subject (e.g. with allative and ablative inflections), but not of inherent sides of objects as opposed to human beings.

74. He also gives *niga* 'south wind', which can hardly have anything to do with Eskimo *nəgəq* 'north wind' (as has been suggested) since it also means 'midday' acc. Radlinski (and may thus go with *kiniulp*).

groups (Evens) absorbing and replacing earlier Yukaghir-speaking tribes.[75] In the section on Chukotian I mentioned the "typical" northern nomadic orientation system of the Evens and Evenk(i)s. It should be pointed out, however, that although the majority of Tungusic groups are still inland reindeer-herders (and it is on their dialects that most lexical material is based), there are some who have settled at river mouths on the Okhotsk coast, and the chief subsistence of these semi-nomadic "maritime" Evens and Evenkis is principally fishing and hunting, like the Nivkh. In fact these groups probably represent "Paleo-Siberians" who shifted to a Tungusic language. Both of the northern Tungusic languages have eastern dialects bordering on the Okhotsk sea between Chukotka and the mouth of the Amur (and on the island of Sakhalin), homeland of the Nivkh, whose territory probably once stretched further north, before the advent of the Tungusic herders.

The basic terms constituting the (eastern) Even system are as follows. There are a number of variations from dialect to dialect (and much intermingling of dialect due to constant movement in the past), but these (taken from Cincius 1975) are typical for the eastern, Okhotsk groups (they appear on Map 9 along with matching terms from a typical eastern Evenki dialect): *n'ūlten tikenmeni* 'west' (lit. 'sun goes down'; Lebedev has *n'oolten tikenmeyin* – compare eastern Evenki *dılačā tikiptin, tikiptu*, etc., of the same meaning); *n'ūlten xīnni* 'east' (lit. 'sun goes up'; Lebedev has *n'oolten hiptun* – compare eastern Evenki *dılačā yūktun, yūktigidēkī, n'ulter, n'ūkte,* from '(sun) goes in'); *iŋen'gīdē* 'north' (cf. *iŋen-* 'cold'; Lebedev also has *hiŋkelten* from *hiŋku* 'dark, night'); and *n'amgīdā* 'south' (cf. *n'am-* 'hot'). Other directional terms in Even (from Lebedev 1982) include *bargida* 'on the opposite side of the river', *buyin* 'away from habitation, into the forest or tundra', and *buygič* 'from the forest or tundra'.

There do not appear to be many specific terms for winds in the lexical sources for these languages, however, which may be due to lack of data or to a lesser reliance on winds in the forested regions of Siberia than further north on the tundra – I have added to the map a single sea wind, *atkilā*

75. This occurred gradually over the last millennium, with Tungusic groups finally reaching all the way along the northern Okhotsk coast – occupied by the coastal Koryaks – in the early 18th century. During the last two centuries they penetrated as far as inland Kamchatka (Aratiunov 1988: 36), where they herd their reindeer on the western side of the central volcanic mountains. The more southerly Evenkis in turn expanded into the lower Amur region and Sakhalin in the 19th century, further reducing the territory of the Nivkh.

(specifically for the Arman sub-dialect). It apparently refers to a west wind further north in the inland Olenski dialect. There is also a cold northern wind *id'a* mentioned for the Aldan dialect of Evenki and also for Even in the standard Evenki dictionary (Vasilevič 1958), in which there are also transparent terms for 'headwind', 'tailwind', 'wind from (off) the river', 'wind from downriver' and 'wind from upriver', presumably likewise found in Even.

These languages also have terms for 'upriver' and 'downriver' (*holla* and *eyeki* respectively in Even), but, like in "reindeer" Chukchi and Koryak, these do not constitute part of the basic orientation system – except in certain dialects, namely the inland (westernmost) Even dialects, where 'north' is 'downriver' and 'south' is 'upriver' (Cincius & Rašis 1952), like in adjacent Kolyma Yukaghir. This is also true of the Bikinski dialect of Nanai on the Ussuri/Amur river system, and – in reverse – in the (southern) Bagruzinski dialect of Evenki, where 'north' is 'upriver' and 'south' is 'downriver'.[76] These riverine systems may represent better the original Tungusic one. The 'north/south' terms of the maritime Evens, referring to the cold north vs. the warm south, suggest influence from Koryak, since both languages refer to the south with a 'warm' term and to the north with a term relating to the cold northern wind. More widespread in Evenki is the distinction between *dolbor* 'north' (or *dolbo-gīdā*, from *dolbo* 'night, dark') vs. *ineŋ* 'day, midday' for 'south' (Aldan dialect), or *tırgan(i)* 'zenith' in the same meaning (e.g. Bagruzinski *tırgan dulin*). None of these appear to use their 'upriver/downriver' terms as referring to up and down coast, however, so there is only slender evidence of a shift from an inland (nomadic or riverine) to a coastal setting.[77]

76. Bikinski Nanai displays a particularly thorough-going riverine system, manifest in its system of spatial adverbs (Sem 1976). This is based on the roots (inflectable in 8 case forms): *duyə* 'upland, towards forest', *vay* 'downland, towards water', *sol'i* 'upriver', *xəi* 'downriver', *baig'i* 'on opposite shore', *ey* 'on this side', *taya* 'on that side' (as well as roots meaning 'up', 'down', 'inside', 'outside', 'behind' and 'in front'). Note that the southern Tungus (to which the Nanai belong) have never been reindeer herders, but like the Nivkh have a traditional economy based on fishing and hunting.

77. But see the section on Fire and Water for the use of 'down' and 'up' terms (with macrocosmic use) to movement towards and away from the fireplace within the traditional "chum" of the Evens (a teepee-like tent), perhaps remaining from the time that semi-subterranean dwellings were still used by the coastal Evens – or their predecessors. Whether there were traces of this also in terms used by the early coastal Koryak – who were pushed northeast by Tungusic herders and then, when resisting the Russian presence in the area, were "subdued" by Cossacks in the late 17th/early 18th century – may never be known since they were displaced eastwards or absorbed too early for linguistic evidence to remain.

To this we can also compare the orientation systems of the two (much endangered) Yukaghir languages, situated to the west of Chukotka in two remaining pockets of a once much larger territory that stretched from the Lena to the Anadyr estuary. Of these, the northernmost group (the "Tundra" Yukaghir) have an orientation system that may reflect their symbiosis with the nomadic Evens, whereas the southern group (the "Kolyma" Yukaghir) displays a purely riverine system, one that may have been original to this isolated language family before the above-mentioned admixture with Tungusic herders, latecomers in the north of their territory.

Nikolaeva (2006) gives the cardinal directions for both languages – plus a couple of forms for extinct Chuvan in the Anadyr basin. The Kolyma system is the simplest to analyze, as it is clearly riverine, based on a north / south axis: *lede* 'downstream, north'[78] vs. *pudi-* 'on top, south' (and related *puidie* 'downstream' – Tundra *purege*). The east / west axis is the same as the Tungusic one described above, i.e. 'sunrise' (*yel'od'əd-ukšibə*) vs. 'sunset' (*yel'od'əd-amluybə*). Oddly enough, this axis is not found amongst the Tundra Yukaghir, despite their closer relation with the Evens. Instead they use two topographically more local terms, *purege-laagar* 'west' (lit. 'upper side', with the same stem as means 'upstream' and also 'south' in the Kolyma language) and *mugid-egiil* 'eastern side of hills', with *mugil* 'row of long hills on the eastern side of the tundra stretching from south to north' and *egii* meaning 'back of the head, space on the east side of the river behind some hills, backwards'. This must refer to the relatively restricted area between the highlands to the west and the flat land around the lower reaches of the Kolyma where they roam (or once roamed). An alternative for 'west' is *saagare* (cf. *sagar* 'side'), given by Nikolaeva as 'west, left side of the yurt (nomadic tent)' (as opposed to *puor* 'right side of the yurt'). Perhaps the sunrise / sunset axis is not particularly strongly associated with the nomadic way of life after all.[79] The converse

78. This term has apparent Uralic cognates, thus Saami and Vogul have **luwe* 'east or south (downstream)', (as opposed to **wilä* 'west or north (upstream)' (the latter originally 'above'). Nikolayeva (1988: 231) relates proto-Yukaghir **le-* 'below' with proto-Uralic **lő-* of the same meaning. The system of the Nganasan Samoyeds on the Taymyr tundra northeast of the Yenisei estuary is described by Dolgix (1962: 292f.) as: 'northeast, down', 'southwest, up', 'southeast' (lit. 'forest side'), and 'northwest' (lit. 'tundra – or sea – side').

79. Orientation by the position of the sun is after all the predominant factor in the absolute systems of Europe among temperate zone agriculturists – cf. Buck (1949 (1988): 868–869). Note that the fact that the 'east' vs. 'west' axis rather than the 'north' vs. 'south' one is sun-oriented here (just as in inland Chukotian) goes against Levinson's claim that such systems usually have a north / south primacy (Levinson 2003: 90).

(geographically determined) correlation may be closer to the mark: peoples of the Arctic coast are unlikely to make use of this axis for absolute orientation, since it is so variable (and indeed absent for part of the year) – but we have seen how the inland Chukchi do nevertheless make much use of it.

The other axis for Tundra Yukaghir is a natural one, namely *yuos* 'north, tundra' vs. either *saa-laagare* 'south' (lit. 'forest side') or *čailed-ord'e* 'south, midday' (as given by Jochelson, based on *čailed* 'daylight' and *ord'e* 'show, appear') – the latter is germane to the 'warmth/daylight' words we have encountered on Kamchatka as well as in Even. Specific to Tundra Yukagir is also the term *iliye-algar* 'lee side' (lit. 'bare of wind'). In sum, the northern system seems both somewhat mixed and somewhat local: it looks as if it could be a riverine one turned inland nomadic (a new category?).

Finally, some remnants are available of the dialect (known as "Chuvan") of the Yukaghir who once lived far to the east towards the Anadyr estuary and were completely absorbed by Chukotians and others in historical times. The two forms given by Nikolaeva for Chuvan do not add much to the picture we have seen already: *emeniy* 'west' is from the stem meaning 'dark', and *pogoy-landywon* 'south' is literally 'warm low place'.

11. Nivkh: fishers and hunters of the lower Amur – and beyond

There is rather detailed information about the orientation system of Nivkh – more so than for most other systems along the Asian side of the North Pacific Rim – thanks to a detailed article by Krejnovič (1986) dedicated to that subject (it covers both the East Sakhalin and Amur dialects – or languages – but focuses on the east at Nogliki) and to the information in Puxta (2003) for the Amur variety, which includes wind terms, not dealt with by Krejnovič. This allows the construction of a combined wind rose plus cardinal direction system of a transparent and systematic nature, as on Map 9, which is specifically for the Amur variety of the language. It can be transferred from the mouth of the Amur to the western shore of northern Sakhalin on the other side of the narrow channel that separates it from the mainland and can easily be crossed by sledge in the winter. This is confirmed by the information in Grube (1892), as collected by Schrenck and Glehn for the Amur and West Sakhalin dialects respectively, where it can be seen that the 'north/south' wind terms in the dialects on both sides refer to the same approximate directions, and that at least one wind (*c'langi* 'side wind') suggests a mirror image west-to-east correspondence across the strait.[80]

Note that the West Sakhalin dialect provided by Glehn is close to the Amur dialect, not to the more divergent East Sakhalin dialect (or language) treated by Krejnovič for the east coast.[81] It is regarded today – e.g. by Gruzdeva (1998) – as going with the intermediate North Sakhalin dialect (which is also close to the Amur variety), so it is indicated on the map by 'Northwest Sakhalin'. For the variety of the eastern language spoken on the Tym River down the centre of the island Krejnovič gives *k'envŋ* '(people) living upriver'

80. However, Mattissen suggests (pers. comm.) that the meaning could be 'cross-axis wind' in the sense of a wind crossing the specified downriver/upriver axis in either direction. Puxta has *člaŋi* 'southwest wind', though it is given by Schrenck for the same Amur dialect as '(south)east wind', and Takahashi (1942) has *tlange la* 'east wind' for South Sakhalin. It is glossed as 'wind from the side' in Saveljeva & Taksami's dictionary.

81. Some groups of Nivkh may already have moved out to Sakhalin over 4,000 years ago according to Vasiljevskij (1981: 92). The division between the East Sakhalin and Amur "dialects" is certainly considerable, but hardly that ancient.

and *anvŋ* '(people) living downstream', corresponding to Amur *k'eqrp'iŋ* vs. *aqrp'iŋ*. This suggests that East Sakhalin is (like Amur Nivkh) essentially a riverine system, with 'upstream' logically to the south. The same applies to the divergent (and now virtually extinct) South Sakhalin dialect of Poronaisk, only with 'upstream' to the north:[82] Takahashi has *kakř* (probably for *keqř*) 'upstream, north', as opposed to *kokř* 'south, down' (cf. the root *qo-* meaning 'down'). These terms are not to be confused with *k'ikr* 'above' – in Schrenck 'inland, towards the hills' (Amur dialect). Glehn gives the 'upstream' term (*keaker* in his rendition) as referring to the north in the West Sakhalin (sub)dialect too, opposite to *konkr (la)* 'south (wind)' (as throughout Sakhalin).[83] The Nivkh of Sakhalin, by the way, call the Amur people *t'aqrpiŋgu* 'those on the opposite side (e.g. of river)', and the latter call the Sakhalin Nivkh *kerqpiŋgu* 'sea dwellers' (cf. Saveljeva & Taksami 1965: 7, who also give *lərmifpiŋgu*, lit. 'dwellers on floating land', as an alternative term). As a *curiosum*, note that the Nivkh regarded Sakhalin as an anthropomorphic figure with a head (at the north end) and stomach, etc. (cf. Levin & Potapov 1956: 778).

The wind rose on the Amur side is supplemented by a set of shore-related terms to form an overall system much like the Northern Wakashan one, but one in which 'into shore' and 'up from the shore (into the woods)' overlap – note that *he-* and *ye-* are regular variants, the latter containing the 3rd person direct object prefix of verbs.[84] The complete set of relevant roots is associated with a set of unrelated verbs of motion, as follows (Amur forms, thanks to Johanna Mattissen):

82. The direction from which the Poronai River runs, the opposite of the Tym. Takahashi also has *tymy-eskn*, lit. 'in the direction of the Tym river', for 'north'.
83. Although Schrenck doubts whether Glehn is correct about the 'north' reading, it could be indicative of the way the upstream/downstream dimension "translates" to the Sakhalin coast directly from the mainland, i.e. the strait between them being treated as a river, much as the Kodiak islanders regard Cook Inlet. More likely, perhaps, is that the situation is simply parallel to the riverine systems elsewhere on Sakhalin – thus Takahashi also has *konrš* 'south wind' and *kokš la/konkř* 'southwest wind' for the South Sakhalin dialect, based on the same root as the 'south' term of Glehn.
84. Puxta distinguishes for the Amur dialect *ye-mid'* 'move up from the shore into the woods' and *he-tX* 'move towards a space close to shore (situated between the shoreline and some point on shore)'. She also gives *he-r* 'close to the shore on water' but *heŋge* 'close to the shore, either on land or on water' (Krejnovič has *hes'* 'on shore by water'). Saveljeva & Taksami (1970) have *yemi-* '(face) towards mountains from the shore', *heqmoq-* 'lie with one's face towards the wall', *heqr* 'area from the shore (or edge) up into the interior', and *her* 'area on the shore between the water's edge and the mountains'.

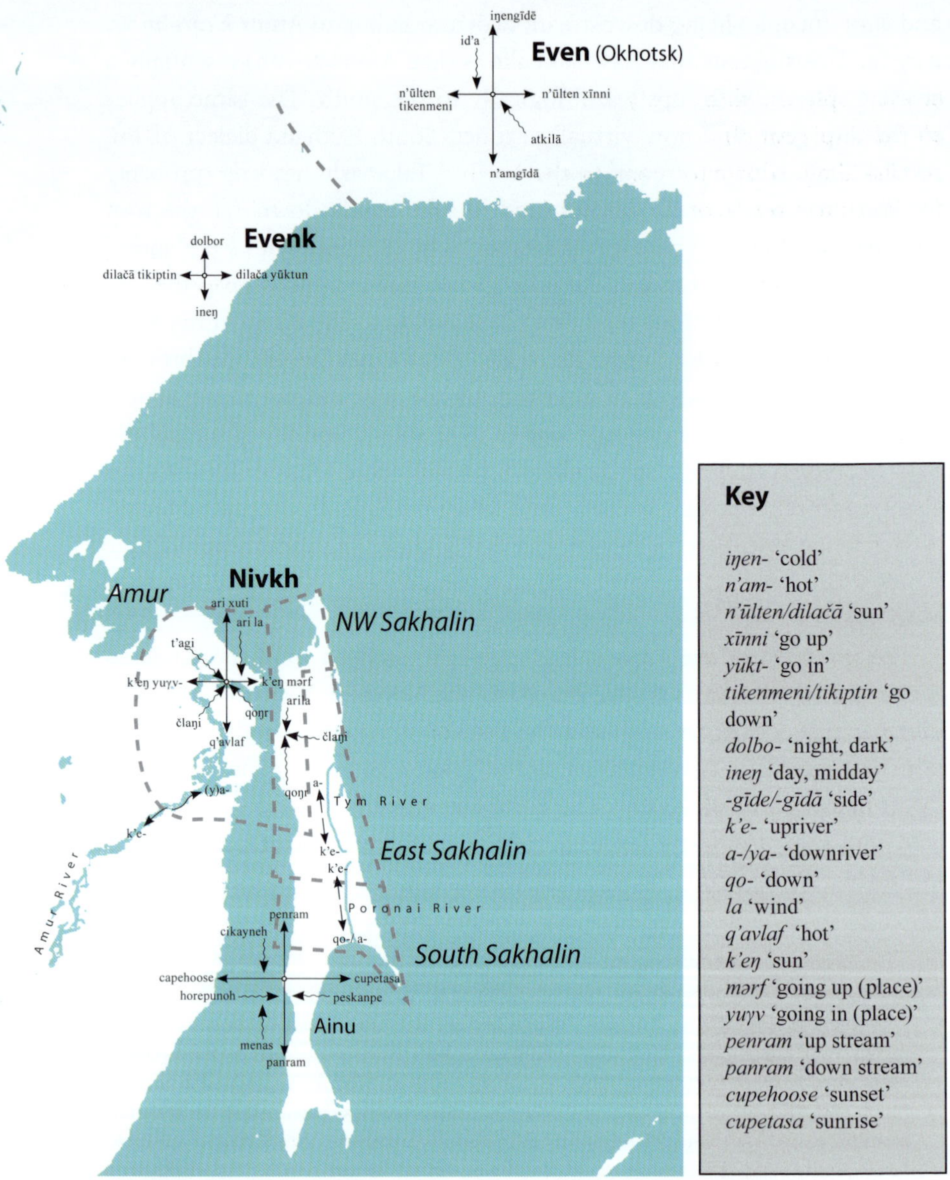
iŋengīdē
id'a
Even (Okhotsk)
n'ūlten tikenmeni
n'ūlten xīnni
atkilā
n'amgīdā
dolbor
Evenk
dilačā tikiptin
dilača yūktun
ineŋ
Nivkh
Amur
ari xuti
ari la
t'agi
k'eŋ yuɣv-
k'eŋ mərf
čłaŋi
qoŋr
q'avlaf
arila
čłaŋi
qoŋr
a-
(y)a-
k'e-
NW Sakhalin
Tym River
k'e-
k'e-
East Sakhalin
Poronai River
penram
cikayneh
qo-/a-
South Sakhalin
capehoose
cupetasa
horepunoh
peskanpe
Ainu
menas
panram
Amur River
Key
iŋen- 'cold'
n'am- 'hot'
n'ūlten/dilačā 'sun'
xīnni 'go up'
yūkt- 'go in'
tikenmeni/tikiptin 'go down'
dolbo- 'night, dark'
ineŋ 'day, midday'
-gīde/-gīdā 'side'
k'e- 'upriver'
a-/ya- 'downriver'
qo- 'down'
la 'wind'
q'avlaf 'hot'
k'eŋ 'sun'
mərf 'going up (place)'
yuɣv 'going in (place)'
penram 'up stream'
panram 'down stream'
cupehoose 'sunset'
cupetasa 'sunrise'

Map 9 Nivkh.

a-/ya- 'downriver' (*qa-d'*)
k'e-/xe- 'upriver' (*tu-d'*)
he-/ye- 'upland, inland' (*maɣ-d'*)[85]
k'i-/xi- 'up' (*mər-d'*)
qo-/Ro- 'down, down to shore' (*məɣ-d'*)
t'a-/řa- 'into river, to opposite shore' (*qo-d'*)

At the core of the system is the upriver/downriver axis, which lies approximately west/east on the lower reaches of the Amur. The most important roots (or stems) concerned are respectively *k'e-/xe-* 'upriver' and *a-/ya-* 'downriver' (the *y-* is the same prefix as on *ye-* above). These items are all extendable by various affixes, e.g. for proximity and "preciseness" – the latter rather like the Eskimo distinction of "extended" vs. "restricted" and Koyukon "specific area" vs. "general area".[86] See Gruzdeva (2007) for an analysis of the actual degrees of proximity involved. Mattissen (2003: 27) lists the nominal derivatives of one root, namely *k'e-*, as follows:

k'er 'precise location upriver (not very distant)'
k'erŋa 'a place upriver nearby'
k'erŋayo 'a place just upriver (from the speaker)'
ek'es 'there upriver'
k'enx 'an extended space upriver'
k'eqr 'distant space upriver, upper part of settlement seen from lower part'
k'eqrŋa 'direction upriver, space upriver nearby'
k'eqrŋayo 'space just upriver'
k'eqrək 'a region upriver far away'
k'eŋgi/k'egi 'from upriver' (cf. *k'eŋgi la* 'wind from upriver')
k'enun 'somebody living upriver'

85. There is a different 'up from the shore' verb corresponding to *he-* in the East Sakhalin dialect acc. Krejnovič (op. cit.: 164), namely *t'eR-nt* (or *t'eɣnt*), also used of moving away from the fireplace to the wall.
86. Compare the suffixes on directionals in Koyukon: *-a* 'heading towards', *-ts'in* 'coming from', *-t* 'specific place', and *-ugha* 'general area' with the corresponding Nivkh suffixes *-qr/kr* '(place)heading towards', *-zuxe* 'coming from', *-s'* 'specific place', and *-nx(e)* 'general area' (*-zuxe* is *-s'* plus the ablative ending). These combine with a similar set of directional stems in both languages (in Koyukon 'upstream', 'downstream', 'upland', 'downland', 'on other side', 'up', 'down', 'inside', 'away', and 'ahead, to centre', and in Nivkh 'upstream', 'downstream', 'upland', 'downland', 'out onto water', 'up', 'near speaker', and 'distant from speaker').

There are also verbal derivatives such as *k'emd'* 's.o. lives upriver', *k'egud'* 's.th. is somewhere upriver', *k'e(ŋ)gid'* 's.th. moves upriver', *xemid'* 's.th. faces/points upriver' and *xet't'* 'take s.th. upriver, carry s.th. from door to back wall of building', and a single adverb *xemi* 'upriver'.[87] These riverine terms can also be applied to objects like houses as in *təv-aqr-k'u-d'* 'it is to the downriver side of the house' (lit. house-downriver-lie-INDIC). Mattissen (pers. comm.) makes the intriguing suggestion that the word for 'sun', *k'eŋ*, could in fact be related to the 'upriver' root, i.e. the direction (roughly south) of the sun and of the upper Amur, in which case there would be a remarkable parallel with the origin of the word for 'south' in Kwak'wala, which, as we have seen, originally meant 'daylight'.

Superimposed upon this are the terms for cardinal directions *ari/are (xuti)* 'north',[88] *q'avlaf* 'south' (literally 'hot place'), *k'eŋ mərf* 'east' (lit. 'place where the sun goes up'), and *k'eŋ yuɣv* 'west' ('place where the sun goes in'), which could be glossed on the neighbouring Tungusic forms of these meanings (as described under "Nomadic and riverine neighbours of the Chukotians"), and/or further influenced by Russian. The remaining intermediate directions are filled in by wind terms from Puxta, namely *qoŋr* 'southeast', *t'agi* 'northwest', based apparently on *qo-* 'down to shore or this side of river' and *t'a-* 'out from shore or to other side of river' (also used of the side of the house opposite the entrance). The "missing" northeast wind is given in Saveljeva & Taksami (1970) as *elvla la* (lit. 'nasty wind') or *řat la* (lit. 'into-the-river' wind). They also have *ŋalvəs* 'southwest wind', *ŋaskarəŋ* 'north wind', and *ŋalɣəvs* 'southeast wind' (the latter corresponding to *ŋalɣuř* in the East Sakhalin dialect – cf. *ŋalagur* 'level with').[89]

87. The root here should not be confused with *ke-* as in *ket* 'east coast of Sakhalin' (Amur dialect), cited by Mattissen (2003: 111) for the South Sakhalin dialect as 'Nivkh living at seashore in South Sakhalin', which is probably related to *ke-řqŋ* 'sea'. Takahashi has *kevn* 'sea-shore dweller', but also *kař eskn* 'east' (lit. 'towards the back'), as opposed to *hukř* 'west', *hokř* 'west coast' (lit. 'area far in that direction' – an indefinite direction in the Amur dialect), and *ketngi* 'upriver (land)' (the latter from *k'e-*, which is *ke-* in the southern dialect).

88. Perhaps related to *əri* 'back', but at all events associated with the cold north wind *ari* (or *ari la* – East Sakhalin *adə* acc. Saveljeva & Taksami); *xuti* is apparently from *k'uti* 'hole' – note that the Nivkh regarded winds as coming through "openings" between the earth and sky in certain directions (Black 1973: 51). But compare also *ari p'rəf* 'place where the aurora appears' (*p'rəf* is lit. 'place where s.th. comes').

89. Takahashi has for the South Sakhalin dialect *ari/adi* (and *lamsi/lamř*) 'north wind' (corresponding to Amur *lams* 'east wind'), *maRi-la* 'south wind' (lit. 'onshore wind'), and *tunkř la* 'west wind' (lit. 'over- this-side wind'?) – *tukr* is 'land on this side of the river' in the

Of particular interest is the parallel way in which Nivkh and Northern Wakashan (and other languages along the Northwest American coast) draw the "macrocosmic" (geographical) world into the "microcosmic" world of the house interior. Unlike in Kwak'wala, the Nivkh house is typically oriented with the door facing downriver, i.e. east on the lower Amur (Black 1973: 8). The stem meaning 'downriver', *ya-*, also refers to the 'lower' part of the house towards the door while the 'upriver' term, *xe-*, also refers to the 'upper' or inner part of the house (or, rather, the sleeping benches arranged around the walls within it). There are, as we have seen, also corresponding verbs (*qa-nt* and *tu-nt* respectively, to give the East Sakhalin forms) for movement in these directions both inside and outside the house. The lefthand side of the house was also distinguished from the righthand side, as in the South Sakhalin forms (from Takahashi 1942): *tairiŋ-if* 'place (bench) on left side when entering the house' vs. *ŋəir(ə)ŋ-if* 'place on right side when entering the house' (with the usual words for 'left' vs. 'right' arm, as in Kwak'wala, though the perspective there is from inside the house looking towards the exit). In the newer "*c'adrəf*" style of multi-family, square-framed house in which most Amur Nivkh lived in recent times (an innovation introduced from further south), the bench to the immediate right of the entrance was called *pal-erq naX* (lit. 'mountain-side bench') and that on the left *tol-erq naX* (lit. 'sea/water-side bench') according to Saveljeva & Takasami's dictionary (1979). The same distinction was made for the separate hearths on these sides of the frame house.

All in all, this suggests an original riverine system with no orthogonal ambiguity between riverine terms as used within the house and outside of it. The only indications of a change due to adaptation to coastal living on Sakhalin (apart from the somewhat doubtful use of the 'upriver' term on the west coast of Sakhalin for 'up the coast' to the north) is the application of the 'down to shore' root to the direction south, especially to a south wind, throughout Sakhalin. Significantly, it is also used for 'downriver' in the South Sakhalin dialect, where 'south' and 'downriver' coincide and where new ways of expressing 'east' and 'west' have arisen (Takahashi's *kař eskn* and *hukř*). The correlation of 'south' with 'upriver' and 'north' with 'downriver' in East Sakhalin is less significant, since it is a natural consequence of the orientation of the Tym river. As with the case of coastal Even and Evenki,

Amur dialect. Glehn has the latter also for West Sakhalin (and Schrenck has *tunyrs* for the Amur dialect).

this overall evidence of a shift of geographical environment is rather weak, but suggestive.

The traditional pattern of life of the Nivkh was that of semi-sedentary, semi-nomadic fishermen who spent the summer months on the coasts near the spawning areas. The earliest Nivkh winter houses (still found on Sakhalin and the Kuriles in historic times) were more or less square semi-subterranean structures, back from the shore or coast, with entrances through the roof, only later replaced by sloping entrance passages (Levin & Potapov 1956: 774). In fact the word for 'come into the house', *təvγ-*, is still transparently *təf/təv* 'house' plus *uγ-* 'come down to' (Gruzdeva 1998: 36). Their summer houses were either on pilings or at ground level, and had small entrances entered by a ladder in front and living space platforms to the sides around a central fireplace (cf. Saveljeva & Taksami 1965: 16). This was also the pattern amongst the Itelmen and Old Koryak people. It may well be that the house-internal terms discussed here reflect the orientation of the winter house not only along the Amur and on Sakhalin, but also far north along the Okhotsk coast before the arrival of the Tungusic reindeer-herding nomads.

Furthermore, the 'onto shore' term also means 'towards the wall (from the centre of the house)' (as well as 'facing the woods/interior'), and the 'down to the water' term also means 'onto the fire' (the fireplace is in the centre of the house floor). Taking a pot from the fire is consequently the counterpart of coming to shore with a boat and also of pulling a net up on shore (*ye-t'-nt* from *ye-/he-*), and putting a pot on the fire is equivalent to pushing a boat out from the shore (*Ro-t'-nt* from *qo-*).[90] This otherwise unusual correlation is parallel with the situation we have seen in a number of the languages of the northern Northwest American coast, in particular Tlingit, Haida, and Northern Wakashan – these share with Nivkh what I call the "fire/water" conflation, to which I devote a separate section to follow. In these languages the fireplace is associated with the "open" dimension ('out at sea', etc.) while the direction away from the fireplace, towards the walls, is associated with the "closed" dimension ('into an enclosed area – the woods or interior, etc.').

The use of the 'upstream/downstream' terms in Sakhalin Nivkh can be compared with those for Ainu spoken until recently on the southwestern

90. This is for East Sakhalin. The *-t'* is from *si-/-t'-* 'put somewhere'. Saveljeva & Taksami (1970) have *Romi* 'direction from the interior to shore, from the top of a mountain to its foot', *Rot'-* 'push a boat out from shore, put s.th. down, take down a pot from the hook (over fire)', which only partially corresponds to Krejnovič's definitions.

coast of Sakhalin, as recorded in Hattori (1964), for there the terms for north and south contain the same words as respectively 'upstream' (*penram*) and 'downstream' (*panram*), only with the initial element *mosiri* 'island, land' replacing *nay* 'stream, narrow valley' in front of it. I take this to indicate local vs. larger region ambiguity. Piłsudski (1998) has *penata* 'upper part of river', *panata* 'lower part of river', also *panke* 'front wall side of the house, person living downstream', and *penke* 'close to the back wall of the house, person living upstream'. This suggests influence from the riverine system of neighbouring Nivkh, which has just this set of oppositions – however, Ainu on Hokkaido is riverine too according to Kirikae's analysis (1993) and has unrelated verbs of motion corresponding to each of its principal directional stems, just as in Nivkh. Note also the alternative expressions Piłsudski gives, *yautoro* 'south', lit. 'dry land side', and *reputoro* 'north', lit. '(out to) sea side', which seem to take Hokkaido as the reference point. As in Nivkh – but also Hokkaido Ainu – it has 'east' and 'west' as 'sunrise' and 'sundown' respectively (*cupetasa* and *cupehoose*). Piłsudski has *cufpokutonne* 'west' (from *cup* 'sun', *pok* 'under', *ut* 'side' and *onne* 'to'), also *cupahun* (with *ahun* 'go in'). Other terms he gives are *makan* 'go landward, away from the sea upwards' (cf. *makun* 'upstream, in mountainous area'), *sapan* 'go towards sea' (cf. *sam* 'go down'), and *yam(ke)* 'go towards land' (cf. *yan* 'land (verb)', also Kurile *yambe* 'upriver'[91]). Hattori adds for Raichishka on the west coast: *peskanpe* 'east wind' ('from the sea shore'?), *horepunoh* 'west wind' ('back wind'?), *menas* 'south wind' (also found on Hokkaido, becoming an east wind in the southernmost dialects), and *cikayneh* 'north wind'. He also distinguishes the front of the house, *sirikaskeke* or *kaske* (lit. the 'upper' or 'right' side), from the back of the house, *siripoh* (lit. the 'reverse' or 'lower' side), with cognates in most Hokkaido dialects.

Much points towards the likelihood that both Sakhalin Ainu and some of the coastal dialects of Hokkaido Ainu represent coastal adaptations of an original riverine system. In fact Kirikae (op. cit.: 114f.) describes a situation in the Honbetsu (western Hokkaido) dialect which is highly reminiscent of the situation of Central Alaskan Yupik at Norton Sound, where a riverine

91. The basic meaning seems to be 'go up'. Pevnov & Urmančieva cite the following related forms for the Saru dialect of Ainu: *yanke* 'land (a boat), take a pot off the fire, put on a stand', *yapte* 'make (s.o.) land or ascend, make (s.o.) take a pot off the fire, make put (s.th.) on a stand', *he-yapte* 'go from the sea to mountains', suggesting that the "fire/water" conflation may extend as far as Hokkaido (though this could be a borrowing in usage from Nivkh).

system has also come down to the coast: according to one of the last speakers of the dialect the verb for moving 'downriver' (*san*) is also used of going to villages south down the coast, and the verb for going 'upriver' (*oman/paye*) is also used of going to villages north up the coast (opposite terms being used for the return journey). Kirikae also cites special terms used in the Pacific coast dialects for 'east' and 'west' (for some, 'north' vs. 'south' acc. Hattori), namely *koy-ka* (lit. 'wave-up') and *koy-pok* 'west' (lit. 'wave-under'), supposedly referring to the Chishima current that flows from northeast to southwest along the eastern side of the Kuriles and Hokkaido. Moreover, he mentions (op. cit.: 117f.) that the "sacred window", traditionally facing upriver within the house, faces east along the southwest coast of Hokkaido, which can be explained by a movement down from inland, where the rivers do actually descend from the east.[92]

By contrast, Kurile Ainu (previously spoken on the Kurile Islands that stretch from the tip of Kamchatka down to Hokkaido) appears to present a second potential "archipelagoan" system in the North Pacific Rim area besides Aleut. In fact the Kurile Ainu called themselves *yaun-aynu*, literally 'shore people' (Vovin 1993: 185), just as the Aleuts call themselves *unaŋan* 'seasiders'. Unfortunately the data here is very limited, but the information in Radlinski's (i.e. Dybowski's) vocabulary for Shumushu, the Kurile island nearest to Kamchatka, suggests a similar "linear" kind of orientation as along the Aleut chain. The terms given are at all events wind-orientated, with an opposition of *venter* 'east wind' vs. *sendruk* 'west wind'.[93] Radlinski also has *očumkampiy sendruk* 'north wind' vs. *rerarki* 'south wind' (the former possibly 'cold wind from behind' – cf. *yampiy* 'cold' – and the latter 'good weather wind' – cf. *reras* 'good weather'). These must surely have been virtually the same on all the islands of the chain, given the probable semantics,

92. Other interesting aspects of Kirikae's study are the partial conflation of the 'up/downslope' vs. the 'up/downstream' dimensions, *san* being used of motion downstream, for example, and *ran* of 'down slope', whereas *ek/arki* is orthogonally ambivalent as between 'upriver' and 'upland', as is another pair of verbs of this kind, *oman/paye* (these originally meant 'cross to this side of river' and 'cross to the other side of river' respectively). These terms are also used within the microcosm, with *san* being used of movement towards the entrance porch (which faced downstream) and *ek* of the opposite (towards the "sacred window"), i.e. parallel with the river. This is the same as in Nivkh, but note that the actual door in the entrance faced towards the river, so there is an inbuilt "orthogonality" in the house layout itself, but one of a secondary kind.

93. The former 'bad' or 'stormy' wind from the sea (cf. *ven* 'bad'), the latter perhaps from *san/sam* 'descend, flow downriver' (but note also *rurusam* 'offshore', lit. 'tide down'). Radlinski generalizes *sendruk* as just 'wind' in some of his forms.

with no coast-relative variation around the individual island coasts. Unlike in Aleut, these terms are not based on demonstrative roots, but neither are they river-related, nor – unlike in Hokkaido Ainu – do the east/west terms refer to the sun's movement (Radlinski has *cup aun* 'sunset' and *cup urikinin* 'sunrise' as separate items). However, the data is, as said, of limited reliability. In fact they seem to reflect the disruptions caused by Russian-controlled sea-otter hunting activities (affecting both the Aleuts and the Kurile Ainu) and the later forced movements resulting from Japanese-Russian hostilities.[94]

More reliable are Hattori's Kurile forms from Shikotan (the southernmost island to which the Kurile Ainu were moved in 1884). He gives for 'upriver' vs. 'downriver' *pet-cha* (lit. 'shore of river') or *yambe* (lit. 'dry land' – referring to Hokkaido?) vs. *pet kucharu* (cf. *pet* 'river' and *kus* 'across river'?), though these are not specifically given in any cardinal sense. If 'upriver' is equivalent here to the direction towards Hokkaido (cf. the use of 'cross river' verbs also for 'go up/downriver' mentioned by Kirikae), this would be the reverse of its direction on Sakhalin. Possibly this could reflect the influence of the Okhotsk Culture that once stretched from southern Sakhalin across northern Hokkaido and up the Kurile archipelago. This maritime (sea mammal-hunting) culture lasted from the 5th to the 13th century and is believed to have been Nivkh-speaking and to represent one strand in the formation of the modern Ainu (cf. Sato et al. 2007), the other one (more inland-oriented) being the Satsumon culture from further south within Japan. Ainu would thus be a relative newcomer to the Kuriles from Hokkaido (under Japanese pressure from the south), as its speakers absorbed or displaced the Okhotsk Culture people that preceded them. At all events, the Kurile dialect was apparently not as distant from those of Hokkaido as Sakhalin Ainu was.

94. At least one of Radlinski's wind terms seems to refer to the direction of Russia, the northwest wind *Sisam sendruk* – from *Sisam* 'Russian' (elsewhere 'foreigner, Japanese') and *sendruk* '(west) wind'. There is also a wind *voyampiy* glossed as 'mainland, continental wind'.

12. Of fire and water

On top of what has been said about the widespread correlation of the use of directional terms within the house (the microcosm) with their use outside the house (the macrocosm), there is, as we have seen, an unusual correspondence in a number of the languages of the North Pacific Rim between the position of the fireplace in the centre of the (bounded) microcosm, the house, and the (unbounded) macrocosmic direction 'out onto the water, into the open' (also the converse, 'away from the fireplace' and 'up from the beach, into the forest'). This is the case both in Nivkh (and possibly Ainu) and, on the opposite side of the North Pacific, Tlingit, Haida, and Northern Wakashan, plus in a few sporadic occurrences elsewhere, which is suggestive of a link of some kind (cultural? linguistic?) across the northern Pacific Rim.[95]

The orientation of the typical Nivkh house is compared in Figure 5 with those of Tlingit and Haida (recall that *he-* and *ye-* are related variants). These schemas can be compared with the orientation of the house in Kwak'wala in Figure 1 (for both riverine and coastal position). Note that over and above the specialized use of the 'down to the shore' and 'in to land' terms in connection with the fireplace, there is also orthogonal ambiguity between the microcosm and the macrocosm as regards the 'upriver/downriver' terms in Kwak'wala but not in the other languages, perhaps reflecting the more complex (and relatively recent) movements within Wakashan territory. All systems showing this "fire and water" correlation display a more complex, secondary kind of "orthogonality", since the direction to or from the fireplace can be to or from either the back or a side wall (where people sit), but probably not from the front, where the entrance is positioned (as shown

95. As regards formal material suggestive of a linguistic link note in particular Haida *q'ad(a)* 'in a clear space, out to sea, onto fire', Nivkh *qo-* 'down to shore, off from shore, onto fire', Tlingit *ʔi·G* 'down to shore' (but unrelated *da·g/de-* 'into open area, out to sea, onto fire'), vs. Haida *diid(a)* 'at/to edge of clear space, landwards, off from fire', (East Sakhalin) Nivkh *t'eR-* 'move up from shore into forest, away from centre of house (fireplace) to wall', Tlingit *da·G* 'back into woods, away from open area, off from fire'. (Note that the apostrophe indicates aspirated consonants in Nivkh, not ejectives.) At present these can only be considered "look-alikes".

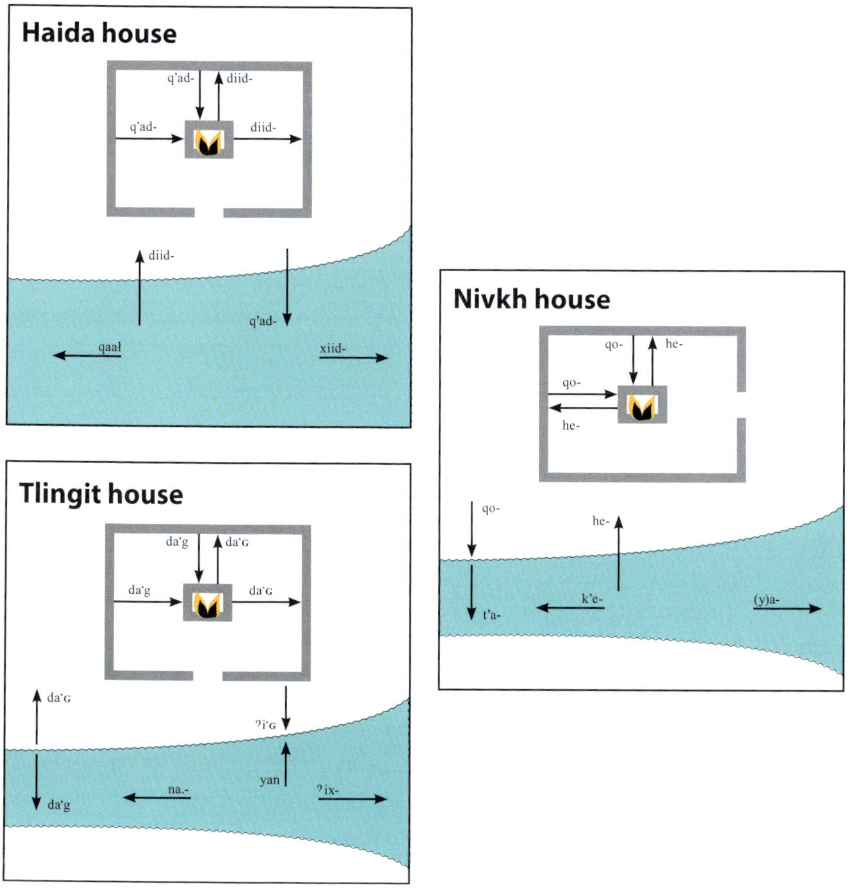

Fig. 5 Directions *vis-à-vis* the fireplace and the shore in three languages.

schematically on Figure 5). This in itself can hardly be taken as indicating a shift from one kind of environment to another in the past – in the case of Haida this is downright unlikely, although it is not impossible that its speakers were once less coastally oriented, with settlements concentrated on the waterways internal to the Queen Charlotte islands. It is also possible that the whole conceptual system was imported from Tlingit along with the numerous lexical loans known to have come that way.

Krejnovič (1986: 165, citing Prokofjev 1935: 11f.) has pointed out the same kind of terminological conflation also among the "Paleo-Siberian" Kets and neighbouring Semoyedic Selkups along the Yenisei river much further west, deep inside Siberia, which is very strange unless this represents the result of early contact with Nivkh.[96] The Selkup forms given by Prokofjev (*karræ* vs. *konnæ*) combine the macroscopic 'down slope (to the river)' vs. 'up slope (from the river)' senses with the microcosmic 'towards the central fireplace' vs. 'away from the fireplace, towards the interior of the dwelling' senses. Note that there is copious evidence of previously utilized semi-subterranean houses with tunnel entrances in the region.[97] To my knowledge there is no evidence of rooftop entrances of the Amuric type here or in the similar structures along the Ob (I shall return to this distinction below).

There has been renewed interest in this phenomenon among the languages of Siberia in a recent paper by Pevnov & Urmančieva (forthcoming) – they discuss it in terms of areal diffusion and contact. Pevnov & Urmančieva give the following meanings for Selkup *karræ* vs. *konnæ* respectively: 'from land onto water, down from shore to water, on water by shore, from woods into tundra, onto the fire, towards the fire' and 'from water to land, up from shore away from water, away from the fire'. For Ket they give *igdæ* 'onto water from shore, down to riverbank from woods, above the fire, at the fireplace, into the fire (or kettle on fire)' vs. *agæ* 'towards the shore from the water, up from shore to woods, into woods, from the fire'.[98] They also find the conflation in Khanty, the neighbouring Ugric language along the Ob, on the far side of the Selkups and Kets. They indicate moreover that the opposition in Selkup, Ket and Khanty refers not only to 'upland' vs. 'downland' but also to 'upriver' vs. 'downriver', which is not the situation in Nivkh but is reminiscent of riverine Eskimo. Given especially the semantics of Selkup *konnæ* ('towards interior of house, upland, up river') I would surmise that we are dealing here with an 'in' vs. 'down' microcosm / macrocosm linkage of the Eskimo type onto which the "fire / water" conflation has been added.

More sporadically, some northern Athabaskan languages display (parts

96. Ket has otherwise a typical riverine system (much like in Kolyma Yukaghir), with 'north' and 'south' being expressed by the same terms as 'downriver' and 'upriver', whereas 'east' is literally 'stony side' and the two alternative terms for 'west' are probably related to 'evening' and 'shore' respectively.

97. One need not go so far as Prokofjev as to talk of living in actual caves, though the Selkup dwellings were indeed recessed into the cliffs, with entrance tunnels down towards the river (cf. Levin & Potapov 1956: 589). The northern Kets lived all year round in tent-like structures (as most of their Siberian neighbours), while the southern Kets had semi-subterranean winter houses, apparently with ground-level entrances (cf. Levin & Potapov op. cit.: 615).

98. They suggest that the opposition *igdæ/agæ* originally referred to the smaller tributaries along which the Ket moved, whereas there are special terms for up and down the Yenisei itself (*tyga* and *uta* respectively), which later became their major axis of transport.

of) this conflation, thus Koyukon has the same derivational prefix string for 'to the shore' and 'away from the fire' (*nee-gho-*), whereas Dena'ina and Lower Tanana conflate 'out into a body of water/an open area' and 'into/towards the fire' (< **nəs-* 'out onto water'), all remnants perhaps of the original pair of conceptual opposites.[99] An independent 'into shore' term distinct from 'up on land' is precisely missing from most northern Athabaskan (as opposed to Tlingit, Kwak'wala and Nivkh) – although Dena'ina and Lower Tanana do have a prefix string (*ni-qa-*) in this sense, not related to the Koyukon above (Kari, pers. comm.).

Furthermore, there appears to be evidence of the same – or a similar – conflation in languages as far afield as at least one Salishan language (close to Wakashan territory) and in certain Tungusic dialects in areas where Nivkh is suspected to have been widespread earlier. In Thompson, a northern interior Salishan language positioned not far from the coast (Kuipers 2002), the opposition is *kʷume* 'upstream, go up away from the water, away from the fire in the winter house' vs. *kʷuce* 'downstream, down towards the water, towards the fire in the house' (< Proto-Salishan **kʷum* 'go up' and **kaw* 'go down' respectively). Note that this conflates the 'downstream/upstream' and 'upland/downland' axes as is typical of Salishan languages. One might speculate that this tribe (like neighbouring Shuswap) was once in closer proximity to Northern Wakashan, now divided from them by Athabaskans.

In coastal (Okhotsk) and Amur watershed Tungusic, the same kind of conflation is also in evidence,[100] namely Even *deed/diin* 'raised side, side opposite the fireplace (in yurt)', *deeski* 'upwards, towards the wall, away from the fire' vs. *ŋeela* 'below, on shore, by the fire', *ŋeen* '(at) shore, edge, lower part, near the fireplace' (and ablative form *ŋeenuk* 'from the fireplace, shore. etc.'). In Evenki the equivalents are *dīlē* 'above, further from the fireplace, nearer the wall' vs. *ŋēskē* 'closer to the fire', *ŋēlī* 'below, closer to the fire'.[101]

99. Koyukon also conflates the meanings 'upstream' and 'rear of the house' (*-naa*), which suggests influence from neighbouring Yupik – see below on the ancient Koyukon house type. Compare this with Dena'ina, which equates 'back wall' with 'upland' rather (*ngge*), and the 'downstream' and 'upstream' walls are homologous with the flow of the river, as expected.

100. Rather surprisingly since it applies to the traditional tent-like *yurt* (or, more accurately, "chum") rather than a more solid sedentary structure – but note that "maritime" Evens did earlier live in semi-subterranean houses like their coastal Koryak and Nivkh neighbours according to Levin & Potapov (1956: 676).

101. Pevnov & Urmančieva also have the opposition here in the senses 'upland, into the forest' vs. 'downland, towards the shore'. They also report this conflation for the nearby

The common factor seems to be 'towards the edge' vs. 'towards the centre' (much as in Haida but expressed here by 'up/down' directionals). It is significant that the Evenki forms are only found in dialects close to Nivkh (including on Sakhalin) or where Nivkh is suspected to have been spoken higher up the Amur river in early times.

The parallelism between the correlation in Nivkh and in the languages of the Northwest Coast of America cannot be so simply explained in terms of proximity or even similarity of geographical surroundings – the cultural factor linking 'towards/away from the fireplace' and 'towards/away from the open sea' seems just too specific (and the geographical similarity between the Amur River and, for instance, the Queen Charlotte Islands not at all apparent). As Nichols (1992: 260) suggests: there is good reason to consider idiosyncratic structural properties of the lexicon as possible "historical markers" (in the broadest sense of indicating *some* kind of historical connection, whether genetic or areal). Enrico (1985) describes the phenomenon for Haida as a conceptualization of the fireplace as the medium of transfer and communication between the (bounded) world of everyday life and the (unbounded) spirit world – offerings to the "Ocean People" (spirits) were made through the fire at the centre of the house.[102] Savaljeva & Taksami (1965: 20) similarly describe the fireplace as having great ceremonial importance for the Nivkh, the spirits of the fire helping man in communicating with nature (e.g. to facilitate the hunt). Certainly the fire and the open water are both places that command respect and awe, dangerous and yet essential for subsistence.

It would not be unreasonable then to suppose that the Amur River in early times represents the source of the "fire/water" correlation. "Amur River ceremonialism" is known to have had an influence on the Old Bering Sea culture over 2,000 years ago around Bering Strait (Ackerman 1984: 118).[103]

southern Tungusic language Udihe. They recreate the original Tungusic roots (**due-* vs. **ŋai-*) as 'upland' vs. 'downland' respectively.

102. Compare the odd conflation in the Northern Wakashan suffix *-(x)tla* 'on fire, on waves, on rounded object', which Lincoln & Rath (no date) generalize as 'on intangible, ethereal thing' (it also refers to 'air, weather' in Oowekyala).

103. Other potential cultural links could be mentioned, for instance the use of labrets by seafaring peoples all around the North Pacific Rim, from Hokkaido to Vancouver Island (and not by interior or Arctic coast peoples of the region). If this is indeed relevant, then the evidence that the use of labrets among the Northwest Coast people started no earlier than about 3000 BC (Carlson 1990: 67) would set a limit on any possible cultural continuum. It would not be incompatible with the possibility that the sea-mammal

This special kind of correlation between microcosm and macrocosm does suggest some kind of North American Coast-Amur Valley relationship. See Dumond (1987: 43 and 49) for the close genetic and cultural links between the Fraser River/Vancouver Island area and Kodiak Island from about 2,500 BC onwards, and for the suggestion that around 4,000 BC this cultural area would have included the Aleutians too. Carlson (1990: 67) has proposed a further, earlier link – via Kamchatka – between the cultures of the Northwest Coast and the coast of the Okhotsk Sea. Note that the correlation as such is not found either in Tsimshian (which has connections further to the south, with the Penutian languages of Oregon) or in Southern Wakashan (where ceremonialism is less developed than in the north), nor can it be reconstructed for Proto-Wakashan.[104]

When one tries to pin-point what it is that all the languages (and cultures) showing this conflation have in common it is tempting to think in terms of the semi-subterranean winter house employed by Neolithic people around the Amur basin and Primorye area at least 4,000 years ago (Levin & Potapov 1956: 38). The Tarya culture of Kamchatka of about the same period also displayed this kind of house. In fact the word for 'door' (*nuc*) in western Itelmen (and recorded in all three historical languages in Radlinski 1891/2 – e.g. as *onoc* in the eastern language) is still rather transparently related to the word for 'smokehole' in Chukotian (*ðəno-*), parallel with the case of the Aleutian word for 'doorway' mentioned in section 7. The source of the phenomenon may actually be still older, going back to late Paleolithic times. (The Anangula site on Umnak Island – then southern Beringia – of some 8,000 years ago apparently shows evidence of such a house type, perhaps also with a roof entrance, though this is by no means certain – cf. Dumond 1977: 43.) There have been many changes of house type and subsistence patterns since,

hunting Ocean Bay culture of Kodiak Island at about this time represents some kind of intermediate link between the Amur region (and Hokkaido) and the west coast of Vancouver Island, on both of which the hunting of whales with harpoons developed at an early stage.

104. Of course it may simply have been lost in the south. Note the supernatural being *tl'e:ʔinwa* given by Sapir for Nuuchahnulth, based on the 'seaward' root *tl'a:-*, also perhaps the suffix *-ħci'i:* 'over the fire' (from *-ħta* 'out to sea' plus *-c'u* 'in a container' and *-(a)yi:* 'give'?). However, it is just as likely that the Northern Wakashans took over the phenomenon from neighbouring Salishans like the Thompson in the Fraser Canyon area – note that Carlson (op. cit.: 67) sees the latter as bearers of the "Pebble Tool tradition" that preceded the arrival of microblade users from Alaska all along the northwest coast.

but enough evidence remains of the old type of habitation – or the transferral of the old kind of "microcosm" to new types – for the idea to be worth following up. What is terminologically in common here is the opposition of a term meaning 'in(to) open space' (e.g. to the fireplace in the centre of the house) vs. one meaning '(out) to the edge of a clear space' (e.g. to the raised platforms around the walls for sitting, sleeping, etc.), as reflected in isolated Haida still today. If there were a central roof-ladder entrance in these old dwellings, the use of a 'down' term to refer to approaching the fireplace, and the use of an 'up' one for away from it (as in Nivkh and Tungusic) would be reinforced (though 'down from / up onto the platforms' might be a sufficient basis). In Tlingit and Northern Wakashan terms meaning 'up onto the land' vs. 'down onto the water' would have served the same purpose.

We appear to be looking then at an "up / down" type of microcosmic orientation, one reasonably linked to the semi-subterranean winter house with roof entrances, as opposed to the "in / down" orientation of the Eskimo-style semi-subterranean house further north with its sunken tunnel entrance down which one had to descend in order to exit the house (a type already found in connection with the earliest Eskimo sites of the Arctic Small Tool tradition – cf. Dumond 1977: 83f.). The approximate distribution of these two types of semi-subterranean house can be seen on Map 10, to which I have added the areas where the "fire / water" conflation is found today (wholly or in part).[105] As can be seen, semi-subterranean houses are not only found all across Siberia as far as Kamchatka and the Arctic coast, as Jochelson already pointed out (Jochelson 1908: 466), but also within Alaska and northwest America as far as the Salishan area where Thompson is located (cf. Mitchell 1990: 348–353 for the Lower Fraser Canyon of British Columbia, where remains of subterranean houses with roof entrances may date back at least 4,000 years).[106] The

105. This is actually a little misleading in so far as the distribution of the Eskimo-style house with tunnel entrance must have been wider at an early stage, since the remains of such dwellings, dated to about 10 or 11 thousand years ago, are found in layer VI at Ushki on Kamchatka according to Dikov (1994: 89), i.e. long before roof-entrance houses appeared there.

106. There were also so-called "pit-houses" in use on the Plateau of Washington and Oregon (and down into northern California) by about 4,000 BC (Fiedel 1992: 124). Plateau groups had already come into contact with microblade users coming down the coast from Alaska at least 2,000 years earlier, so this house type could also have arrived that way. The pit houses of the early agriculturalists of southwest America are another matter. They are both later and their idea believed to have diffused down from the north rather than from Meso-America (Josephy 1973: 156).

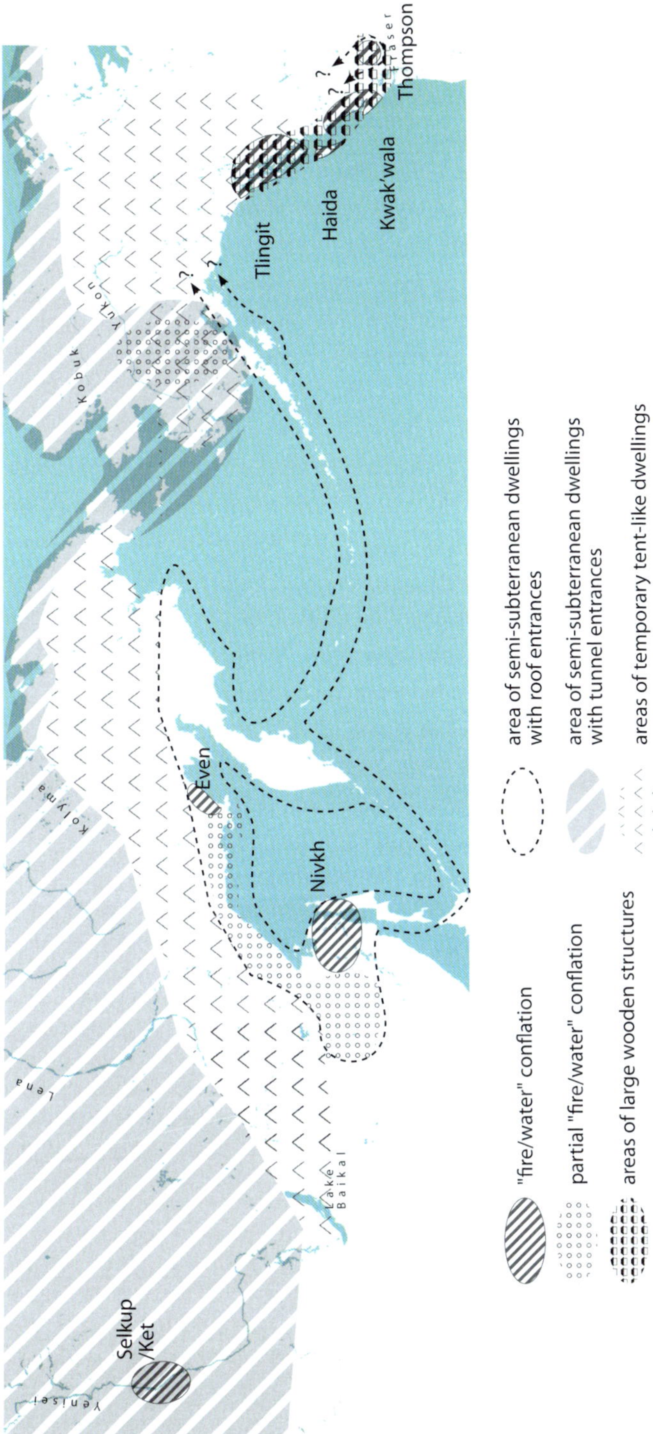

Map 10 Earliest house-forms.

break between Thompson (Salishan) and the Eskimo-Aleut area is filled by the typical wooden structures of the Northwest Coast tribes, where wood suitable for building large structures is abundant and much of the earliest archaeological record is in any case below sea-level today.

The Eskimo type house persisted until recent times in the dwellings of the maritime Chukchi as well as of the Eskimo themselves along the Arctic coasts. It may in fact represent a direct line of descent from the Paleolithic type of house found on the Angara river at sites like Buret' at least 10,000 years ago, which displayed an entrance tunnel leading down towards the water (Levin & Potapov op. cit.: 17), the type also found in the early semi-subterranean dwellings of the Semoyedic Selkups.[107] Moreover, the traditional house of the Koyukon, near the mouth of the Yukon, and probably other Athabaskan groups situated close to Eskimo territory and strongly influenced by them, was of the Eskimo type (Jetté & Jones 2000: 810). Note that in the ensuing "Mesolithic" Sumnagin period in Siberia this house type – which may be traceable back to the Dyuktai culture of the mid-Lena / Aldan region of eastern Siberia[108] – largely disappeared (along with the hunting of megafauna on the open tundra), to be replaced by the tent-like "chums" of nomadic forest hunters. However, "dug-out" dwellings appear again in the Neolithic of the Lower Lena and Kolyma (believed to reflect the ancestors of the present-day Yukaghirs – Levin and Potapov op. cit.: 789).

This all suggests different diffusion routes for the two types of house, with the Amur valley being the source of the (later) roof-entrance type and of the "fire / water" conflation that goes with it, although the Angara and Baykal sites could represent the common source of both. Note that the headwaters of the Amur (with its extension the Shilka) and the Yenisei do not lie very

107. This could be indicative of an ancient Uralic-Eskimo link, as has many times been suggested in the past, including by myself (Fortescue 1998). It assumes that the southern Ket took over the house type and orientation of their Selkup neighbours. However, it may well be that the phenomenon goes back to a common "Paleo-Siberian" past that included Ket.

108. This has been identified in turn with the Paleo-Arctic tradition of Alaska (and Beringia), which is considered by some to reflect the origins of the Na-Dene people, but at all events probably points back to much earlier sites near Lake Baykal. There is some evidence of semi-subterranean dwellings dating from at least 10 thousand years ago at Berelekh on the Arctic coast en route between the lower Lena and Alaska (Fiedel 1992: 38). Dyuktai lasted from approximately 18 to 10 thousand years ago, and the microblade tradition with which it is associated reached Kamchatka about 11 thousand years ago and the present Tlingit area of southwestern Alaska by about 9 thousand years ago – see Fortescue (1998: 183ff.) for a summary.

far from each other, almost connecting via Lake Baykal and the Angara. As regards the Aleuts (who had the roof-entrance kind of house but lacked the "fire / water" conflation), they may well have brought their Eskimoan microcosmic terminology with them when they absorbed or ousted earlier people they met on the archipelago whose house style they eventually took over. In time they altered the basic Eskimoan system in their own idiosyncratic manner.[109]

The extension of the microcosmic directional terms would arguably everywhere have been outwards, towards the macrocosm, the result varying somewhat according to geographical setting – but the house type itself would in turn have depended strongly on the macrocosmic setting, so the relationship must be characterized as "bidirectional". The "fire / water" conflation phenomenon appears neither to be specifically maritime nor inland-oriented, but simply indicative of a certain widespread perspective on the relationship between microcosm and macrocosm in early hunter-gathering societies of this vast northern region. For the time being the exact source (or sources) of the phenomenon must remain a mystery, one that is strangely fitting for a survey of orientation systems around the northern Ring of Fire.

109. I am assuming (as most archaeologists appear to today) that the earlier Anangula site, which already had semi-subterranean dwellings, was pre-Aleut, as was the Kodiak tradition of the southern Alaskan coast, which also may have had similar houses, though the evidence is not very clear. The Eskimo house type was at all events brought down to the Pacific coast during later Norton tradition times (Dumond 1977: 66f.).

13. Conclusions

I summarize in Table 2 my findings for the principal languages dealt with in this survey. The five types indicated in the third column (along with shifts from and to them) are (1) riverine, (2) coastal, (3) nomadic, (4) archipelagoan, and (5) "large island". Items in parentheses indicate very old stages at or beyond the limit of reconstruction, or newer ones only just beginning to become established. The other columns indicate various "anomalies" that may be diagnostic of shifts from one type of geographical location to another, namely: an orthogonal relationship between the same terms used for the microcosm (within the house) and the macrocosm (around the house) – "orthog.1"; ambiguity of the same terms used in a coastal and a riverine sense – "orthog. 2"; other kinds of anomalies – "other anom.";[110] ambiguity between local and broader "regional scale" usage of the same terms – "local ambig."; and the conflation of terms for 'towards/away from the shore' and 'towards/away from the fireplace' – "fire". The last two categories are not really diagnostics of shifts as such: local vs. regional ambiguity is a factor common to most of the systems looked at (perhaps only excepting the nomadic ones), and the "fireplace/water" conflation is an unusual, superimposed dimension in its own right. As explained earlier, a particular type of shift does not preclude a still earlier shift in the other direction (this is particularly true of Eskimo and Northern Wakashan languages). Uncertain cases (mainly due to lack of data) are indicated by question marks and marginal manifestations of a trait are in parentheses.

110. By "other anomalies" I mean cases like the oddity of the Eyak 'downriver/upriver' terms, the break-up of the downriver/upriver axis in Interior Tlingit, the directional vs. wind-related senses of *ejgə /ayval* in Chukchi, the breaking of the outside/inside axis in macrocosmic usage in CAY Eskimo, and the (re)alignment of the microcosmic house wall axis with the macrocosmic coast-oriented axis in Barrow Inupiaq.

Table 2 *Orientation types*

Family	Language	Type	Orthog. 1	Orthog. 2	Other anom.	Local ambig.	Fire
Wakashan	Nuuchahnulth	2				(x)	
"	Kwak'wala	2 → 1	x	x		x	x
"	Haisla	(2 →) 1	x	(x)		x	x
Tsimshianic	Sm'algyax	1 → 2		x		x	
"	Nisga'a	1				?	
isolate	Haida	5				(x)	x
Na-Dene	Tlingit (coast)	1 → 2		x		x	x
"	Interior Tlingit	2 → 1		(x)	x	?	?
"	Eyak	1 → 2		(x)	x	?	
"	Dena'ina	1 → 2		(x)			(x)
Eskimo-Aleut	Alutiiq	1 → 2	x	x		x	
"	CAY (Bethel)	(2 →) 1	x		x	x	
"	CAY (Kotlik)	1 → 2	x	x		x	
"	Inupiaq (Kobuk)	1	x	?		x	
"	Inupiaq (Barrow)	1 → 2			x	x	
Eskimo-Aleut	Naukanski	(1 →) 2	x			x	
"	CSY (Chaplino)	2				x	
"	Aleut	4					
Chukotko-Kamchatkan	Chukchi (maritime)	3 → 2			x	x	
"	Chukchi (reindeer)	3					
"	Koryak	3 (→ 2)			x	?	
"	Alutor	(3 →) 2	?			(x)	
"	Itelmen (western)	1	?	?			
Tungusic	Even (Okhotsk)	3 (→ 2)			(x)		x
"	Evenki (eastern)	3 (→ 2)			(x)		(x)
isolate	Nivkh	1 (→ 2)		(x)		x	x
isolate	Ainu (Sakhalin)	1 (→ 2)		(x)		?	?

The principal kind of "shift diagnostic" indicated here is still that expressed by the "orthogonality hypothesis", which I presented in preliminary form already in the Introduction. But note that there are now two varieties of this, as distinguished by "orthog.1" and "orthog. 2" in the table. I need to adjust my original formulation accordingly. Let me rephrase it this way: unambiguous systems with "dedicated" terms forming two orthogonal axes applied to an essentially coastal or riverine setting – and with a direct homologous correspondence of these terms to their usage within the house (where this applies) – will, all else being equal, probably be "original" (i.e. very old), whereas ones in which there is ambiguity (with at least some terms being used in two different, more or less orthogonal senses) will have adapted to new geographical circumstances within a not too distant past. Such anomalies may not always distinguish between movement from a coastal setting to a riverine one as opposed to the reverse, and, moreover, a change in house type (without necessarily any great geographical shift) might itself produce an anomaly, although in such cases there is likely to be an associated change in subsistence pattern and/or influence from newcomers with a conflicting system. Recall also what was said in the previous section about the earlier house types on the Aleutians and in the Yeniseian region, which may have been taken over by people bringing different kinds of orientation systems with them. In complex cases such as that of coastal vs. inland varieties of Northern Wakashan or Alaskan Eskimo, in which several successive phases have succeeded one another, one may have to draw upon what is known about the etymology of the terms concerned or about the (pre)historic background of the population, and this may be complicated by periods of only seasonal presence on the coasts or river banks. It is helpful to specify the *degree* (or extent) of ambiguity in such systems, since it appears that riverine systems brought down relatively recently to the coast display more ambiguity (and orthogonal "breaking") than ones that have long since adapted to the coast – even if one suspects that these must themselves have come down from inland at some remote period.

There are, however, some cases in Table 2 where there are no (or only marginal) orthogonal diagnostics indicated and yet where one can be reasonably sure of shifts of environment in the not too distant past. Most of these display "other" kinds of anomaly (as discussed above), and this includes coastal Even and Evenki, where one suspects replacement of the riverine terms found in inland Tungusic dialects by non-riverine terms influenced by neighbouring coastal Koryak.[111] Moreover, as we have seen, there are also strong traces of the "fire/water" conflation there – itself a kind of anomaly reflecting in all probability the earliest form of semi-subterranean dwelling in the Amur/Okhotsk area – since general terms for 'down' vs. 'up' are also used of microcosmic movement towards or away from the fireplace, and

111. The special case of Alutor (and other "maritime" Koryak) has been dealt with in section 8 on the Chukotian systems.

'near fire' terms also refer to macrocosmic 'at the shore'. A general caution is nevertheless in order here: the diagnostics adduced in the table are not infallible, merely indicative.

Now, as mentioned at the outset of this investigation, Levinson (2003) would characterize all of the orientation systems represented along the northern Pacific Rim and adjacent Arctic regions as crucially embodying "absolute" frames of reference, defined by fixed bearings of one sort or another (albeit "resetable" from one large-scale region to the next). He suggests that such systems may be typical of hunter-gatherer societies (op. cit.: 212).[112] However, there is a great deal of variation within this overall type, and it can indeed be questioned whether type (2) in Table 2, the purely coastal type typified by coastal Eskimo, is really "absolute" in the way he defines this term, although he does distinguish a "sub-absolute" landmark sub-type of absolute system, which would cover both the coastal and riverine Eskimo systems, for example (op. cit.: 314f.). This is to be distinguished from the more canonically absolute "cardinal" sub-type (op. cit.: 66).[113] The problem is that a coastal system (at least in the region we have focused on) will typically incorporate more than one type of "landmark" in any given locality, e.g. prevailing winds – which can be rather stable in a larger (e.g. dialect) area – as well as the coastline itself, which may shift absolute direction (along with the terms indicating left or right along it) quite significantly, even at the local level. Potential ambiguity may thus arise between local and more regionally stable senses of the same directional terms (note that wind and coastal directional terms in Eskimo languages largely share the same roots). Levinson does discuss differing "scales" or circumstances of use at which the same system can be reinterpreted at different levels of abstraction (op. cit: 49). He also describes hybrid systems such as that of Bali (op. cit.: 132), where

112. But see Majid et al. (2004) for a cross-linguistic study that concludes that there is little evidence for "ecological determinism", apart perhaps for the tendency for urban dwellers to use relative systems where rural dwellers use absolute ones.

113. His more formal definition of an "absolute frame of reference" is as follows (op. cit.: 50), where F = Figure and G = Ground: "Absolute relator R expresses a binary relation between F and G, asserting that F can be found in a search domain at the fixed bearing R from G. The origin X of the coordinate system is nearly always centred on G and the system of terms anchored by reference to a conceptual 'Slope' S. G may be any object whatsoever, including ego or another deictic centre; F may be a part of G." A "relator", note, is a term expressing a relationship between F and G, and the "Slope" of a fixed bearing system projects infinite parallel lines across environments. G in the case of coastal Eskimo would, for instance, be the coastline.

a fixed "cardinal" monsoon wind axis is combined with an 'up towards the central mountains' "landmark" axis that changes as you move around the island coast. The Inuit coastal system would seem, however, to combine more radically a "landmark" absolute system with a "relative" system (i.e. relative to the right and left side of the speaker looking out to sea).[114] This system also contains numerous instances of "mirror-image" relations across bodies of water, a matter of "reflection", which Levinson sees as typical of relative systems (op. cit.: 49). He does mention (op. cit.: 108) that absolute systems may have some marginal relative interpretations (e.g. 'uphill' in Tzeltal may refer to 'higher up' in the viewer's field of vision), but in coastal Eskimo this lies at the core of its "absolute" system, in which **ug-* and **kiv-* are *always* interpreted in an observer-relative sense along the coast.

It is in general unclear within Levinson's theoretical framework how one is to categorize languages that superimpose more than one distinct "absolute" system, whether this is a matter of a local and a more regional one, as in most Eskimo, or of situations where local "landmark" terms have become influenced (and eventually reinterpreted) by the cartographically fixed cardinal bearings of a dominant language like English or Russian. It is also unclear whether there is as sharp a boundary between "cardinal" and "landmark" systems as Levinson envisages. Cardinal systems – if one takes the standard European languages as exemplars (cf. Buck 1988: 868–869) – are typically reliant on the position of sunrise and sunset, and yet the precession of the sun across the sky is itself a "landmark", one that varies seasonally through time just as coastal landmark systems vary through space. The distinction between the two can at all events not simply be equated with the difference between hunter-gatherers and other kinds of society (nor does Levinson suggest this): many of the "landmark" systems that have been touched upon in this study incorporate the movement of the sun as a major axis, notably those of the interior Chukotko-Kamchatkan and Tungusic languages, Ainu, Tsimshianic, some Yukaghir and even some eastern Eskimo (though only the most southern varieties of Arctic Quebec and Labrador), all of which have hunter-gatherer backgrounds. It seems natural enough to

114. Though recall that in coastal Eskimo these are not expressed with the words for 'left (hand)' and 'right (hand)', which are principally used of the human body unless extended by affixation (e.g. with a personal suffix 'my/your/his' to refer to a direction projected out from a specific human body). They are thus not used of inanimate objects, although these may have intrinsic 'front' and 'back' sides like humans (typically with a distinction between 'area in front/behind' and 'front/back side of s.th./s.o.').

combine such an axis with another that is linked to some more "grounded" local landmark, whether it be a river, a coast, a mountain range or a prevailing wind.[115] The advantage of such "hybrid" systems is presumably that they allow variation on one axis while maintaining relative fixity on the other over a broader geographical area – as with the Balinese system mentioned above. Less "natural" is the situation where the one of two crossing axes has distinct interpretations (orthogonally related or even diametrically opposed) depending on context, as we have seen happening for example in Northern Wakashan. In analyzing such situations it is essential to draw upon the relationship between the geographical "macrocosm" and the house-interior "microcosm", a relationship which Levinson mentions as characteristic of languages of the Arctic (op. cit.: 81), but does not elaborate.

The results of the present investigation do mesh nicely, however, with the suggestion in Burenhult & Levinson (2008: 144f.) that languages display "semplates" (for "semantic templates") in their orientation systems, i.e. prefabricated cultural systems that cut across a number of semantic and linguistic domains – in our case apparently also across language boundaries. "Semplates" correspond to broad "cultural models" and take their starting point in different baselines or "leitmotifs", such as motion, part and size, or part and containment. In the languages we have looked at along the North Pacific Rim the most widespread manifestation of such entitities would appear to lie in the general microcosm/macrocosm linkage, but this also covers more culturally specific cases such as the "Fire/water" conflation in Northern Wakashan, Tlingit, Haida and Nivkh. The semantic domains cut across are the interior of the house and the surrounding geographical environment (including movement back and forth between the two).[116] The linguistic domains cut across vary from language family to family – in the case

115. I have not even considered orientation by the stars in this investigation, though this may be as important for Arctic travellers in certain situations as navigation by terrestrial landmarks (cf. MacDonald 1998: 160-191 for a fine description of how the Igloolik Inuit make use of this in combination with other indices of direction in a largely flat region of the high Canadian Arctic). Bogoraz (1904–9: 307–314) has a description of the stars and constellations significant for Chukchi orientation.

116. There is a further, secondary extension to the parts of the boat or canoe in some of the languages concerned (cf. for example Krejnovič op. cit.: 165 as regards Nivkh, and Leer 1989: 576 as regards Na-Dene). In Eskimo languages note that *ug-* 'down' vs. *kig-* 'outside' can be extended in derived forms to the human or animal torso (the lower/back vs. upper/front half) – the use of *kig-* here (rather than *kiv-* 'inside') may be due to influence from another derivative **kigayəg* 'shoulder blade'.

of Haida and Kwak'wala, for example, the basic opposition is expressed both by directional stems and by (unrelated) suffixes, and in Tlingit both by directional nouns and preverbs. Compare too the essential "leitmotif" of 'up' vs. 'down' in many of these languages (especially on the Asian side) with that of the Eskimo-speaking world, where the leitmotif from which the dominant "semplate" is generated is 'inside' vs. 'down' rather.

One should be cautious, however, about applying the notion of an overarching microcosm/macrocosm semplate across the board to all Arctic and sub-Arctic languages (a generalization it is tempting to make). As we have seen, there is no overlap between house-internal and house-external uses of the same terms in Tsimshianic and Southern Wakashan,[117] but this is also true today of most forms of Inuit Eskimo in Canada and Greenland, where the terms that still overlap in Alaska have become gradually separated and specialized (only the overlap in the meaning of *kilu* 'rear wall, inland' remaining in some dialects). It is also unclear to what degree – if any – "maritime" Chukchi has maintained the linkage found in inland "reindeer" Chukchi for the designation of the different walls of the *yaranga* in the context of modern house types. Perhaps then "pure" coastal systems tend not to develop this linkage – or tend to shed it easily. The 'out to the open sea' direction is after all uni-directional, whereas the interior sides of the house face each other, like the banks of a river.[118] Only Central Siberian Yupik seems to go against the tendency – and this coastal language, it should be recalled, was probably brought from the Alaskan side of Bering Strait, where a riverine microcosm/macrocosm linkage developed at an early stage. The generalization definitely does not apply to the "large island" and "archipelagoan" variants of the coastal type of system attested in Haida and Aleut respectively (if they really are variants). In the case of Aleut it may be (as we have seen) that the application of the original Eskimo-Aleut coastal system to a new house type (and geographical setting) was the catalyst for the development of its

117. Nuuchahnulth *-aqtlił* 'down coast' does contain *-ił* 'inside the house', but as Sapir (1938: 257) suggested, the earlier meaning of this may once have been more general, perhaps 'in a closed space', as opposed to *-is* 'on the beach', which may have meant 'in an open place', reminiscent of the principal spatial opposition in Haida and Tlingit.

118. This further suggests a logical source for the fire-water conflation: the 'confined/enclosed' vs. 'out in the open' axis ('up in the woods' vs. 'out to sea' in the macrocosm) could become interpreted within the two dimensional microcosm as the interior walls of the house folded, like a bay, around the open floor with the fireplace at the centre. Perhaps this semplate is after all more likely to develop in maritime settings – or on the shores of very wide rivers – as a variant of the general microcosm/macrocosm linkage.

particular microcosm/macrocosm linkage, whereas in Haida the "fire/water" conflation (the essential linkage in that language) may have been due to influence from Tlingit, imported along with the lexical loans known to have come that way. Haida is at all events clearly an integral part of the Northwest Coast cultural area and its speakers are known to have travelled far and wide along the coast.[119]

At this point we must leave it to the cultural anthropologists to eke out further explanations involving the importance of the house and its focus, the hearth, in the Arctic and Sub-Arctic worlds. It should be recognized that we may ultimately be confronted with the kind of purely cultural relativism, largely free from environmental determinism, that adheres to Burenhult's and Levinson's notion of the "semplate". One area which it might be fruitful to investigate for further evidence linking choices of frame of reference to the specifics of hunter-gatherer ways of life is that of time as opposed to space, for here there is less scope for purely cultural variation. Evans (2009: 314ff.) has suggested that there may be distinct temporal frames of reference akin to the spatial ones, namely "event-based" and "experiencer-based" frames, where the former perspectivizes an event in terms of its sequential relation to a reference event (like a spatial landmark), independent of the speaker's perspective, while the latter corresponds to deictic tense, i.e. future, present and past from the speaker's point of view.

The question relevant to the present study is this: do languages that favour a "landmark" spatial frame of reference – which, with the caveats discussed above, includes all of the languages of the study – also favour a particular temporal frame of reference? Levinson (2003: 262) hints at such a correlation in connection with the absolute system of Tzeltal. An initial impression as regards the languages of this study is that they may well reflect a consistent preference: all display complex distinctions of aspect but the only experiencer-based tense category found everywhere is future, and future is as much a matter of epistemic (or deontic) modality as it is of tense as such.[120] Typi-

119. In fact, the microcosm/macrocosm linkage is lacking in the languages of some of the groups in the survey with the *least* mobility outside of their own territory, for instance the inland Tsimshianic and (probably) Itelmen tribes.

120. The only exceptions, where the choice between morphologically expressed past, present and future tenses is obligatory, are the Tungusic languages (nomadic late-comers to the region from the southwest), Aleut and Itelmen (both of which have come under strong influence from Russian and are highly endangered), and North Slope Inupiaq (where English influence is strong).

cally, the distinction between past and present is made by implicature from the use of aspectual categories in context (perfective often being regarded by default as indicating the past). Perhaps more importantly, most of the languages – if not all – use the same terms for 'in front' and 'first, before, ancestors' on the one hand, and 'behind' and 'last, after, descendants' on the other, an "event-based" (sequential) perspective that seems natural for people with a "landmark" perspective on space. But this is a different story – our spatial one must for the time being end here.

Appendix 1: The languages of the survey

As we have seen, the grammatical framework of a language has a direct bearing on its means of expressing spatial orientation. Below I give a brief characterization of the languages (or language families) with which this survey is principally concerned, limiting myself largely to those traits relevant to the expression of orientation. This covers salient aspects of both syntax and morphology, and to a much lesser degree also of phonology. As regards the latter let it suffice to state generally that all the languages lie on an approximate continuum from complex phonology (with large inventories of phonemes and complex morphophonemic alternations) in the east, to simpler phonological systems in the west.[121] Of course there are some divergences from this – such as the complex morphophonemic alternations of Nivkh on the Asian side (the phonemic inventory of that language is nevertheless rather simple). Although all of the languages are relatively "synthetic" (if not extremely polysynthetic), there is great variety in their typological profile – and in the ways in which they express spatial relations.

1. *Wakashan*

a) *Southern Wakashan* (Makah, Ditidaht, and Nuuchahnulth/Nootka)

These languages are characterized by polysynthesis of the purely suffixing, single stem kind, with a wealth of derivational suffixes, notably in the form of several hundred "lexical suffixes" with greater semantic weight than suffixes in more familiar languages. Lexical stems include a handful of important "empty roots" to which lexical suffixes must be attached (if not to some other stem). Some lexical suffixes are verb-like, "incorporating" a noun-like stem. Inflectional categories are loosely organized, with suffixes (or clitics) of person, number, tense and mood rarely being obligatory (and 3rd person regularly marked by Ø). Clitics of modality and mood, etc., are attached in a templatic order when required and can "migrate" as a whole to position following the first lexical item in the sentence. The distinction between parts

121. The complexity is at its extreme in the Wakashan family – which also displays complex reduplication processes – and at its simplest in Ainu.

of speech is notoriously fluid (and this extends to the functioning of some classes of lexical affixes). There are classificatory verbs chosen according to the shape of objects, an "inverse" suffix on verbs, and no case marking on nouns.[122] Spatial relationships are expressed principally by lexical suffixes, of which over a hundred refer to spatial orientation and movement, but there is also a limited set of stems referring to spatial orientation not tightly integrated into sub-systems. Word order is basically VSO, though the choice of what element in the sentence is chosen as predicate ("V") is very free, and there are, as expected, some (few) prepositions.

b) *Northern Wakashan* (Kwak'wala, Oowekyala, Heiltsuk, and Haisla)
The Northern Wakashan languages differ from those of the south (to which they are rather remotely related) especially in the realm of inflectional categories: these are more paradigmatically rigid in the north and involve combinations of demonstrative / deictic elements in subject, object or instrumental / possessive function. For the third person this includes the distinction of 'near speaker', 'near addressee' and 'distal' (all with corresponding 'invisible' counterparts). These elements are obligatory on nominal arguments and present a wide array of choices according to prenominal and postnominal position, sometimes (especially in Heiltsuk) requiring marking of more than one such category in succession, and (in Kwak'wala) often with a shift of proclitic elements to the preceding lexical constituent (becoming enclitic upon it). There are both intransitive and – by simple addition of object suffixes – transitive verbal paradigms (the latter peripheral or residual in Southern Wakashan). Word order is basically VSO, as in the south, but with an even greater tendency to chose items not obviously verbal (e.g. adverbs and conjunctions) to fill the "V" slot as sentential predicate.

2. *Tsimshianic* (Coast Tsimshian / Sm'algyax, Gitskan, and Nisga'a)
These languages are somewhat less polysynthetic than the Wakashan ones, and their polysynthesis is of a different nature, involving canonical noun incorporation rather than lexical suffixes. They are also less generally "head-marking" than neighbouring languages and are morphologically ergative as regards

122. Most of these features are also shared by Chimakuan further south on the Olympic peninsula. The Southern Wakashan languages differ from neighbouring Coast Salish languages mainly by lacking their prefixes, gender distinctions, and obligatory marking of referring noun phrases by articles / demonstratives, and by displaying a wider range of lexical suffixes (those of Salishan languages are mainly body part terms).

pronominal affixes (but display no case marking on nouns). There are few suffixes but a wide array of proclitics, many with spatial meaning comparable in variety to the Wakashan spatial suffixes. Obligatory marking of nominal expressions by demonstrative/deictic elements ("determiners") is reminiscent of Northern Wakashan (and Salishan), but not so obviously spatial in nature (it involves, unusually, the distinction between common and proper nouns). Subject markers are either prefixed (to active verbs) or suffixed (to static verbs) like object markers. There are complex means of forming the plural of nouns (involving reduplication), and both numeral classifiers and (some) classificatory verbs. Word order is VSO and there are a number of (spatial) prepositions.

3. *Haida*

Although not very polysynthetic or head-marking (with neither lexical suffixes or noun incorporation) Haida does have a good many derivational suffixes – including a number of important ones with spatial meaning. Some of the main orientation terms are independent stems, however. It also possesses numerous proclitics but these are primarily of an "instrumental" nature. It has tense/aspect/modal suffixes, but does not have any pronominal subject/object affixes on verbs. It has classificatory verbs and several other traits in common with Na-Dene, including – unlike any of the languages named so far – SOV word order and both simple and complex postpositions. It also has a stative/active distinction in its pronominal marking, though neither grammatical nor local case (or possessive affixes) on nouns.

4. *Na-Dene*

a) *Tlingit*

Like all Na-Dene languages, Tlingit displays a templatic kind of polysynthesis with dependency relations between verbal stems and preceding prefixes or adverbial "preverbs" that often affect stem shape (although this is not as extreme as in related Athabaskan). Also like the other Na-Dene it has SOV word order with postpositions despite being primarily prefixing. Unlike the languages listed so far, it has a tightly organized sub-system of directional expressions. This consists of a closed set of stems taking specific affixes and postpositions (and with a specific derivational potential), plus a number of "preverbs" (overlapping with the set of directional stems). Nominal stems are otherwise rather simple (and lacking in case markers), but there are possessive prefixes, like in all Na-Dene. It has both numeral classifiers and (some) classificatory verbs, and only very limited noun incorporation.

b) *Eyak*

Eyak has many of the distinctive traits of other Na-Dene languages, but relies on semi-independent "preverbs" still more than Tlingit does (rather than the Athabaskan type of derivational prefix chain). Its directional expressions also form a sub-system like that of Tlingit – though not as clear-cut as in the latter. This involves overlapping preverbs and postpositional expressions that are either simple or combinations of a directional stem and a further postpositional suffix.

c) *Dena'ina (Athabaskan)*

Dena'ina is very similar in typological profile to all other northern Athabaskan languages in displaying a high degree of head-marking and a proliferation of prefixes and discontinuous "derivational strings". Many of these are spatial in nature, comparable to Wakashan lexical suffixes (see Appendix 2). There is incorporation of both nouns and postpositions. Successive prefixes are combined in single complex verb forms according to an overall morphological template. Verb stems vary in shape for tense, aspect and long-distance dependencies from preceding prefixes. Also subject and object pronominals are in the form of prefixes. There are much-used classificatory verbs reflecting the shape or consistency of objects. In the verbal morphology there is an "inverse" (rather than passive) distinction. Besides individual preverbs and postpositions of a spatial nature, Dena'ina has a special sub-system of spatial expressions much like that of Tlingit, consisting of demonstrative prefix, directional stem and case suffixes (allative, locative and ablative). The latter are not found on ordinary nominal expressions, which are very simple. Number marking on nouns in particular is very limited, as in all Na-Dene (and Haida).

5. *Eskimo-Aleut*

a) *Yupik*

Like all Eskimo-Aleut languages, the Yupik languages of Alaska and Chukotka are highly polysynthetic – of the purely suffixing, single-stem kind. They are not as head-marking as neighbouring languages of Alaska and Canada however, in so far as they display full sets of case suffixes on nouns (both grammatical – ergatively organized – and local). The morphology is recursive, with possible shifts from verbal to nominal or the reverse several times in one complex word (verbal or nominal). Though Eskimo languages contain an impressive number of derivational suffixes these do not include "lexical suffixes" of the Wakashan kind, directional meanings being expressed rather by a large array of demonstrative roots (probably the most fine-grained of any language family in the world), each with parallel adverbial, pronominal and deictic forms. They also display a restricted number of "relational" stems, all of which can be inflected for local case, like nouns.[123] Verbs take paradigmatic sets of portmanteau suffixes for mood (subordinate as well as main clause), person and number (for both subject and object), all other suffixes between stem and inflection being optional – and that includes "sentential" suffixes of tense, modality and polarity. There is also a 3rd/(reflexive) 4th person switch reference alternation in both nominal and verbal inflectional paradigms. The word order is rather free, with mixed SOV and SVO patterns, and a distinction between plural and dual is maintained throughout all paradigms. There is a clear distinction between nominal and verbal stems – the only other category is "particle" (adverbial or conjunctional).[124]

b) *Inuit*

The Inuit continuum of dialects differs very little from Yupik as regards core morphosyntax. There is an even greater number of derivational suffixes (both verbalizing, nominalizing and valence-preserving), but a somewhat reduced array of demonstratives the further east one goes. As with Yupik, there are no postpositions as such, their function being taken over by case-inflected nouns and "relational" stems ('above', 'below', etc.) – also by "applicative" constructions on the verb. Derived participial forms of verbs may, as in Yupik, either be inflected as nouns or be integrated into verbal mood paradigms; in North Alaska this also involves a tense distinction.

c) *Aleut*

Aleut is somewhat less polysynthetic than Eskimo, in so far as it has fewer productive suffixes and makes much use of auxiliary verbs (corresponding to "sentential" suffixes in Eskimo). Its means of expressing direction and location is nevertheless much like that of Eskimo, relying heavily on a similar array of demonstrative roots and "relational" stems that can be extended by local case inflections. The word order is predominantly SOV (like Inuit dialects further east than Alaska). One egregious difference from Eskimo is the breakdown of the morphological ergativity of Eskimo and its reformulation

123. Which further mark pronominal possessor, forming portmanteau morphemes of number, case and person.
124. Siberian Yupik has a considerable number of free particles borrowed from Chukchi (sometimes replacing the sentential suffixes found elsewhere in Eskimo languages).

as a system of "anaphoric reference", emphasizing topicality of reference rather than transitivity.

6. *Chukotko-Kamchatkan*

a) *Chukotian* (Chukchi, Koryak, Kerek, and Alutor)

Unlike Eskimo, these closely related languages are both prefixing and suffixing and indeed make considerable use of a number of derivational and inflectional circumfixes. They are still less head-marking than Eskimo, containing fairly elaborate case systems on nouns (though without a genitive case), but are nevertheless highly polysynthetic in the extent to which productive (and recursive) incorporation – both of nouns and adjuncts – dominates their morphology. Vowel harmony of a bi-directional "root retraction" type helps maintain the integrity of complex words. They lack the wide array of demonstrative roots of their Eskimo neighbours, relying more heavily on individual lexical stems for directional expressions. There are complex verbal mood/tense/aspect paradigms (for subject as well as object person and number, as in Eskimo), which includes traces of an earlier "inverse" system based on a person hierarchy (1st person highest). There is a class of adjectival stems with distinct inflectional/derivational potential, and a wide range of modal/pragmatic "particles". Word order is rather free, with (some) postpositions. Much use is made of auxiliary verbs (both intransitive and transitive), and dual is distinguished from plural on verbs as well as nouns – with the notable exception of Chukchi. All nouns may be marked as "singulative" too, either by suffixation or reduplication, and animacy is an important dimension in nominal inflection patterns. The syntax is ergatively organized (there is a distinct ergative case on nouns), but this is not transparent in the morphology of (most) verbal paradigms.

b) *Itelmen*

Distantly related Itelmen differs on many counts from the Chukotian profile given above. It is far less polysynthetic (with no incorporation at all), although it shares most of the inflectional categories and paradigms expressed by prefixes and suffixes in the Chukotian languages. It has been greatly influenced by neighbouring Koryak/Alutor, and the exact nature of its relation to the northern branch of the family is controversial – since only one variety of a much wider range of dialects/languages remains it is hard to judge the original situation before contact with Russians and Koryaks. It also lacks ergativity (there is neither ergative nor accusative marking on nominal arguments), with more rigid word order (predominantly SVO) partly making up for this. It does have a similar (and related) array of local case suffixes on nominals as its Chukotian neighbours, and these applied to locational/directional stems like 'upriver' or 'downriver' constitute the core of its directional system. It has nouns marked for plural and singulative number and also has both applicative and anti-passive affixes on verbs, just like Chukotian. Vowel harmony of the Chukotian sort is only residual, but telling.

7. *Tungusic* (Even and Evenk)

The northern Tungusic languages are typologically very close despite being spread (in countless intermingling dialects) across a vast area of western Siberia. They are typical agglutinative, suffixing SOV languages with postpositions and vowel harmony of a root-retracting (but – unlike Chukotian – unidirectional) kind. They display somewhat less morphological elaboration than the languages discussed so far, although they have a good many derivational suffixes, including verbalizing ones of the Eskimo-Aleut kind (quasi-incorporating). Like the latter family they also have a morphological passive and indicative paradigms based on participles (subordinate clauses are non-finite or expressed by converbs). They have auxiliary verbs for the expression of mood/tense/aspect,[125] also for negative polarity (which is morphologically expressed in most of the other languages of the survey). They display nominative/accusative orientation, marking accusative case. Nouns also take a rich array of local case suffixes and are marked for plural number (but not dual) and possessor (plain 3rd vs. reflexive suffixes, following case), although a genitive case on nouns is lacking. Adjectives are noun-like, and there is agreement between head nouns and modifiers. Verbal inflection is simple (intransitive only, by suffix).[126]

8. *Nivkh*

Nivkh displays a somewhat unusual kind of polysynthesis, which Mattissen calls "dependent-head synthesis". It consistently fuses adjuncts and object arguments with following head constituents (such as a transitive verb) triggering complex phonemic alternation patterns at morpheme boundaries

125. As opposed to the valency-changing and verbalizing auxiliaries of Chukotian.

126. Yukaghir falls in a number of ways somewhere between Chukotian and Tungusic, differing from the latter mainly by the presence of adjunct (but not noun) incorporation, by its lack of auxiliaries, its only marginal vowel harmony, its genitive marking on nouns, and transitive as well as intransitive verbal paradigms.

that vary according to word class.[127] There are no adjectives distinct from verbs, and transitive verbs are distinct from corresponding intransitive ones principally by having initial fricatives rather than plosives. The word order is predominantly SOV, with postpositions and suffixes (though some personal pronouns are prefixed). Despite the high degree of synthesis there is surprisingly little inflectional morphology in the language, with no subject person marking on indicative mood verbs at all. There are, however, numerous focal and modal suffixes (applicable in a distinct order) and various subordinate "converb" forms of verbs. Though it has nominal cases suffixes, these do not include a distinction between nominative and accusative case (nor is there a genitive case), and plural marking is in many situations optional. Its extensive system of numeral classifiers (fused with numerals) is distinctive, as is its closed system of "landmark roots", involving a small number of spatial roots with specific derivational potential, reminiscent of the situation in Na-Dene.

9. *Ainu*

Ainu is also polysynthetic and head-marking, with incorporation (recursive even), applicative derivations, transitive as well as intransitive verbal paradigms, and both prefixes and suffixes, but with far simpler morphophonemic processes binding successive morphemes together than in the other polysynthetic languages we have seen. It has SOV word order and postpositions, also mood/tense/aspect auxiliaries, reciprocal and antipassive/indefinite object prefixes, and numeral classifiers (much like Nivkh in these respects). It lacks the noun case inflections of its neighbour, however, and number (plural) marking is still more peripheral than in Nivkh.

127. Also residual vowel harmony is involved in such alternations.

Appendix 2: Directional affixes and clitics in the languages of the Northwest Coast

The languages of the Northwest American coast (and hinterland) are well known for their highly differentiated arrays of affixes or clitics expressing spatial direction, location and movement. These are not only highly differentiated but also (given their morphological status) at least to some degree grammaticalized. Even within the Wakashan languages, which display the highest number of such morphemes, they are not actually obligatory, however, only textually far more frequent than would be expected from European languages.

Directional/locational morphemes actually represent only a part of the broader array of "lexical" affixes and clitics that typify most of these languages. Some, like Haida, have a large number of instrumental proclitics, for example, but relatively few purely spatial suffixes. Athabaskan languages (represented here by Koyukon of the lower Yukon) have a large and varied array of prefixed/interdigitated "derivational strings", of which many are of a spatial nature (comparable in number with Tsimshianic proclitics), but these tend to have a more abstract (though sometimes highly specific) "path" sense and are generally – as expected – less geared to coastal locations. It is useful to compare the distribution of morphological means of expressing spatial meanings across semantic parameters in the different language families of the area (not least because it might reveal areal factors at work). However, it should be borne in mind that the absence of morphological means of expressing a particular meaning does not mean that the latter is not distinguished at all in the language concerned – thus, for instance, certain basic meanings such as 'above' and 'below' are expressed in Koyukon by lexical means (directional roots) rather than by affixes. Nevertheless, the fact that a particular meaning is expressed by morphological rather than lexical means must have some significance for the frequency with which the notion concerned is expressed.

As mentioned, the highest concentration of such morphemes is to be found among the Wakashan languages – of the several hundred lexical affixes listed by Sapir and Boas respectively, Nuuchahnulth has approximately 130 (75 appear in Table 3) and Kwak'wala 71 (65 in the table) devoted to purely spatial meanings.[128] Only a portion of these relate to natural features of the environment, however (and are thus liable to be integrated into local "orientation systems"). Tsimshianic also has a large array of such items (43 in Table 3), rivalling Wakashan, whereas Haida and Tlingit further north have a more restricted number of affixes / clitics (Eyak even fewer, perhaps surprisingly given its relationship with the spatially prolific Athabaskan languages).[129] Further south the number of such morphemes peters out rapidly with the Salishan languages – which display many lexical affixes (epecially those related to body parts) but few of a purely spatial nature[130] – but return again in some profusion further south with the Hokan and (some) Penutian languages of Oregon and northern California. Also Chimakuan Quileute, just south of Makah, has a large array of lexical suffixes very similar to the Wakashan.[131]

The semantic contents of these items overlap and vary in specificity, so it is actually rather hard to say exactly how many semantic features are distinguished. What one can do is to sort these out into certain "basic" reoccurring meanings. They fall into about 16 groups (depending on how you deal with the overlap), which cover the types of meaning that are commonly expressed morphologically across the region. These are: (1) orientation *vis-à-vis* the beach, (2) orientation *vis-à-vis* the sea, (3) orientation *vis-à-vis* the woods / forest, (4) orientation *vis-à-vis* the river, (5) orientation *vis-à-vis* water (surface), (6) orientation *vis-à-vis* a slope / hill, (7) orientation *vis-à-vis* the

128. The high number in Nuuchahnulth has both to do with the detailed coverage of affixes in this language but also with the fact that many of them conflate path and location meanings with other more specific "ground" elements. The lower number of items indicated in the table than in the sources also reflects the fact that more than one morpheme may correspond to a given gloss in the table.
129. As regards Tlingit, Story & Naish (1973) list a number of directional items (particles) immediately preceding the verb complex that are associated with prefixes and stem changes within the complex itself, much like the "derivational strings" of Athabaskan languages. Eyak too has its "preverbs".
130. Thus for example Upper Halkomelem (Galloway 1993) has around 100 lexical suffixes, of which only 6 are of a locational / directional nature (in the meanings 'in a circle', '(on) ground', 'location round a house', 'end of house', 'side', and 'upright'. These are almost exclusively used in nominal compounds.
131. These include *-wa* '(on the) beach', *-yaX* '(on) rock', *-tłoł* '(on the) ground', *-t'si* 'in the water', *-sp* '(on the) fire', *-c'il* '(on a) platform', *-t'co* '(on the) river bank', *-łi* '(at a) cape, point of land', and *-la'q* '(on the) coast' (from Andrade 1933). Other items with counterparts in Wakashan languages include 'side of a canoe', 'the sky', 'gravel at bottom of sea', 'territory', 'river', 'hill' and 'top of a bag'.

coast, (8) orientation within/around the house, (9) orientation *vis-à-vis* the fireplace in particular, (10) orientation *vis-à-vis* a canoe/boat, (11) geometrical (topological) dimensions, (12) gravitationally defined dimensions, (13) general types of motion, (14) type of surface, (15) dimensions over barriers, and (16) other (natural) landmarks.[132] Clearly there is some semantic overlap between the individual categories, but the divisions chosen, although overlapping, are all internally coherent and potentially expressed independently in any given language of the area. These major semantic categories can be divided (across category) into those expressing static location, those expressing path or direction towards, and those (a smaller number) expressing direction away from some landmark (this should be clear from the glosses).

Whereas some languages will have individual morphemes of a fairly general, broad meaning, others will divide up the relevant semantic area more finely. In some instances there are notable conflations of categories, for instances directions within the house and directions orientated towards the river or the coast, found in many languages of the area, or more culturally specific ones like the conflation of direction to and from the fireplace with to and from the open sea that I have focused upon. Some languages regularly distinguish location (at) and direction (to or from) by different inflections (e.g. Tlingit), whereas others may have unrelated affixes for all of these (e.g. Nuuchahnulth). Moreover, some very general morphemes of an abstract geometrical meaning can be used in more specific contexts, such as a general 'out of' affix being used in some languages also for 'out of the house' whereas other languages distinguish these meanings with separate items, or an affix referring basically to a body part can be used in an extended/metaphorical sense, as when 'into the mouth' can also be interpreted as 'into an inlet' in certain but not all languages of the area. There are also obvious overlaps involved in meanings like 'away from the beach', which is virtually the same in the context of the Northwest American coast as 'up into the woods' – only construed within a slightly different frame of reference.

The following table should give a general impression of how these meanings are expressed morphologically across selected languages of the area

132. For comparison, note that Davidson (2002) divides up Sapir's Nootka suffixes relevant to space into "Path-orientation" (53 items), "Nature" (14), "Geometric" (44), and a handful of "miscellaneous" suffixes containing spatial elements. Dunn (1999) analyzes the locative proclitics of Tsimshian (10 "Stative" and 20 "Motion" items) according to the abstract semantic dimensions 'internal vs. 'external'; 'tangent' vs. 'non-tangent'; 'above' vs. 'below'; 'proximate' vs. 'remote'; 'parallel' and 'perpendicular'.

(Nuuchahnulth, Kwak'wala, Nisga'a, Haida, Tlingit and Koyukon), though certain reservations are due, partly because of the varying quality of the dictionary glosses of the items concerned, but also since the exact border between what is to be considered as purely "spatial" and what is not is not always easy to draw (and the criteria may vary somewhat from language to language). Also, the "same" meaning is sometimes expressed by more than one affix/clitic in a given language (although they may differ subtly) and this is not indicated. It is also of course more than likely that I have simply missed out items that should have been added to the table for individual languages since they are lacking in the sources I have available. Affixes/clitics that cover both orientation to the shore or sea and orientation towards the fire(place) or wall have, exceptionally, been marked under both categories.

A perusal of the table will show that there is considerable variation from language to language as to which specific spatial meanings are expressed morphologically: there is little sign of common areal patterns emerging apart from a handful of core meanings which have obvious environmental significance such as 'upriver' vs. 'downriver', 'out to sea' vs. 'in to the shore', etc. Of greater significance is the morphological profile of the languages themselves – it comes as no surprise that languages with a very high number of lexical suffixes (like Nuuchahnulth) will also have a high number of suffixes with a spatial meaning. Sometimes the same meaning can be expressed either morphologically or lexically (by unrelated morphemes), as, for example, 'upriver' and 'downriver' terms in Kwak'wala. This is especially true of the Wakashan languages, whose concern for precise spatial meanings was characterized by Boas (referring to Kwak'wala) as an "exuberant development of localization" (Boas 1911: 445).

Table 3: *spatial affixes/clitics*

Type		Nuuch.	Kwak.	Nisg.	Haida	Tling.	Koy.
1) orientation *vis-à-vis* beach	down to beach/shore	x	x	x	x	x	x
	on beach	x	x				
	up from shore	x	x	x	x[133]	x[133]	x
	along shore	x	x	x		x	

133. In generalized sense 'into closed-in space/to edge of open area'.

Type		Nuuch.	Kwak.	Nisg.	Haida	Tling.	Koy.
2) orientation *vis-à-vis* sea	seawards	x	x	x	x		
	to shore	x	x	x	x	x	x
	on sea	x	x				
3) orient. *vis-à-vis* woods	into the woods	x	x	x	x[133]	x[133]	x
	out of woods	x	x	x	x[134]	x[134]	x
	in woods	x					
4) orient. *vis-à-vis* river	on bank	x	x				
	downriver	x	x	x		x	x
	upriver	x	x	x		x	x
	at river/bay mouth	x	x				
5) orient. *vis-à-vis* water	in/under water	x	x	x	x		x
	on water	x	x				x
	into water	x	x				x
	to surface of water	x					
6) orientation *vis-à-vis* a slope	down slope	x		x		x	x
	up slope			x		x	x
7) orient. *vis-à-vis* the coast	down coast	x	x				
	up coast	x	x				
	in bay	x					
8) orient. around house	in house	x	x				
	out of house	x	x	x	x		
	on roof	x	x				
	in front of house		x				
	into house	x	x	x	x		
	at head of bed	x					
	at wall	x					
	away from wall			x			
	at rear of house	x		x			
	round back of house			x			
	in centre of floor	x					
	at door	x	x				
	on ceiling	x					

134. In generalized sense 'into open space'.

Type		Nuuch.	Kwak.	Nisg.	Haida	Tling.	Koy.
9) orient. *vis-à-vis* fireplace	on fire	x	x				
	into fire					x	x
	towards fire		x[135]	x	x[135]	x[135]	
	away from fire		x[136]	x	x[136]	x[136]	x
10) orient. *vis-à-vis* a boat	into boat				x		x
	in boat	x	x				
	at stern of boat		x				
	at bow		x				
	at side of boat	x					
	on gunwhale	x					
11) geometrical dimensions	underneath	x	x	x			
	above	x	x	x			
	in middle	x	x				
	out of hole		x				
	into hole	x	x				
	through hole	x	x				
	in(side)	x	x	x		x	x
	in corner	x	x				
	on top of	x	x	x			
	on top of long standing thing		x				
	at end	x	x	x			
	at hole in top end	x		x			
	between	x	x				
	in front of	x	x	x			
	behind	x	x	x			
	on side of	x	x				
	alongside	x					
	at vertical surface	x					
	at end of	x	x	x			
	at base of	x					
	at summit	x					
	outside			x			x
	flat against	x		x			
	from centre to edge						x

135. Conflated with 'out onto the water/sea'.
136. Conflated with 'towards the shore/up into the woods'.

Type		Nuuch.	Kwak.	Nisg.	Haida	Tling.	Koy.
	into centre						x
	in a line			x			x
12) gravitational dimensions	down	x	x	x	x	x	x
	up	x	x	x	x	x	x
	down over drop-off						x
	up from ground	x					
13) general types of motion	away	x	x	x			x
	around		x	x			
	towards goal	x	x	x	x		x
	apart	x	x				x
	out into open	x	x[137]	x	x[137]	x[137]	x
	into interior	x	x[138]	x	x[138]	x[138]	x
	back			x	x		
	past	x	x	x			x
	looping in semi-circle						x
14) type of surface	on rocks	x	x				
	on ground	x	x				
	on flat thing	x	x				
	on long object		x				
	on round object	x	x				
	on raised platform	x					
	on fabric-like surface	x					
15) over barriers	opposite		x				x
	across	x	x	x			x
	across hill		x				
	barring passage			x			
	across strip of land				x		x
	across body of water				x		
16) other landmarks	at point of land	x	x				
	on cliff/buff	x		x			
	in sky	x					
	into valley						x

137. Conflated with 'out of the woods' and/or 'seaward'.
138. Conflated with 'into the woods' and/or 'to shore'.

Sources

Wakashan

Boas, F. 1911. The Kwakiutl Indian Language. In: F. Boas (ed.) *Handbook of Native Indian Languages,* Part 1, 423–557. Washington: The Smithsonian Institution.

Boas, F. 1924–25. A revised list of Kwakiutl suffixes. *IJAL* 3, 117–131.

Boas, F. 1934. *Geographical names of the Kwakiutl Indians*. New York: Columbia University Press.

Davidson, M. 2002. *Studies in Southern Wakashan (Nootkan) Grammar*. Ph.D dissertation, State University of New York, Buffalo.

Dick, Mary Jane. (Typescript, no date.) Ahousaht Dictionary.

(First Voices: Kwakw'ala, at www.firstvoices.ca)

Fortescue, M. 2007. *Comparative Wakashan Dictionary*. München: Lincom.

Grubb, D. 1977. *A practical writing system and short dictionary of Kwakw'ala (Kwakiutl)*. Canadian Museum of Civilization Mercury Series, Canadian Ethnology Service Paper no. 34. Ottawa: National Museums of Canada.

Lincoln, Neville, and John Rath. 1980. *North Wakashan Comparative Root List*. Canadian Museum of Civilization Mercury Series, Canadian Ethnology Service Paper no. 68. Ottawa: National Museums of Canada.

Lincoln, Neville, and John Rath. 1986. *Phonology, Dictionary and Listing of Roots and Lexical Derivates of the Haisla Language of Kitlope and Kitimaat, B.C.* Canadian Museum of Civilization Mercury Series, Canadian Ethnology Service Paper no. 103. Ottawa: National Museums of Canada.

Lincoln, Neville, and John Rath. (Typescript, no date.) North Wakashan suffix dictionary.

Nakayama, Toshihide (ed.). 2003. *George Louie's Nuu-chah-nulth (Ahousaht) Texts with Grammatical Analysis*. Endangered Languages of the Pacific Rim A2-028. Suita: Faculty of Informatics, Osaka Gakuin University.

Rath, John. 1981. *A Practical Heiltsuk-English Dictionary with a Grammatical Introduction*. National Museum of Man Mercury Series, Canadian Ethnology Service Paper no. 75. Ottawa: National Museums of Canada.

Rose, Suzanne Maria. 1981. *Kyuquot Grammar*. Ph.D. dissertation, University of Victoria.

Stonham, John. 2005. *A Concise Dictionary of the Nuuchahnulth Language of Vancouver Island*. Lampeter, Ceredigion: The Edwin Mellen Press.

Salishan and Chimakuan

Andrade, M. J. 1933. Quileute. In: F. Boas (ed.) *Handbook of American Indian Languages*, vol. 3, 152–292. Washington: The Smithsonian Institution.

(First Voices: Nuxalk, Sliammon, and Sechelt, at www.firstvoices.ca)

Galloway, B.D. 1993. *A grammar of Halkomelem*. Berkeley: University of California Press.

Kuipers, Aert. 1969. *The Squamish language, grammar, texts, dictionary*. The Hague: Mouton.

Kuipers, Aert. 2002. *Salish etymological dictionary*. Missoula, MT : Linguistics Laboratory, University of Montana.

Nater, H. F. 1984. *The Bella Coola Language*. Ottawa: Mercury Series, National Museums of Canada.

(Saanich Classified Word list, at www.lingtechcomm.unt.edu)

Tsimshianic

Anderson, M.S. *Sm'algyax Living Legacy Talking Dictionary* at www.smalgyax.unbc.ca

Boas, Franz. 1911. Tsimshian. In: F. Boas (ed.) *Handbook of American Indian Languages*, Bulletin No. 40, part I, 283–422. Washington: Smithsonian Institution.

Dunn, J.A. 1995. *A practical dictionary of the Coast Tsimshian language*. Seattle: University of Washington Press.

(First Voices: Nisga'a and GitsenimX, at www.firstvoices.ca)

Sasama, E. 2001. *A descriptive study of the Coast Tsimshianic morphology*. Ph.D. dissertation in Linguistics at Kyoto University.

Tarpent, Marie-Lucie. 1987. *A Grammar of the Nishga Language.* Unpublished Ph.D. dissertation, University of Victoria.

Haida

Boas, F. 1891. Vocabularies of the Tlingit, Haida and Tsimshian languages (ms. at www.canadiana.org/view/14308/0013)

Enrico, John.1985. Fire as the conduit to the other world: a note on Haida deixis and Haida belief. *International Journal of American Linguistics* 51, 400–402.

Enrico, J. 2005. *Haida dictionary*. Fairbanks: Alaska Native Language Center.

Lawrence, Erma. 1977 (typescript). *Haida dictionary*. Fairbanks: Alaska Native Language Center (also at www.eric.ed.gov/ERICDocs/data/ericdocs2sql).

Swanton, J.R. 1911. Haida. In: F. Boas (ed.) *Handbook of American Indian Languages*, Bulletin 40, Part 1, 205–282. Washington: Smithsonian Institution.

Tlingit

Boas, F. 1891. Vocabularies of the Tlingit, Haida and Tsimshian languages (at www.canadiana.org/view/14308/0013)

Leer, J. 1989. Directional systems in Athapaskan and Na-Dene. In: E.-D. Cook & K.D. Rice (eds) *Athapaskan Linguistics*, 575–622. Berlin/New York: Mouton de Gruyter.

Leer, J., D. Hitch, and J. Ritter. 2001. *Interior Tlingit Dictionary*. Whitehorse: Yukon Native Language Center.

Story, Gillian L. and Constance M. Naish. 1973. *Tlingit Verb Dictionary*. Fairbanks: Alaska Language Center.

Story, C.L. and C. M. Naish. 1976. *English-Tlingit Noun Dictionary*. Revised by H. Davis and J. Leer. Sitka: Sheldon Jackson College.

Wrangell, Ferdinand von. 1839. Word list supplement from his *Beitrage zur Kenntnis des Russischen Reichs*. St. Petersburg (available on Internet).

Athabaskan-Eyak

Jetté, Jules and Eliza Jones. 2000. *Koyukon Athabaskan dictionary*. Fairbanks: Alaska Native Language Center.

Kari, James. 2007. *Dena'ina Topical Dictionary*. Fairbanks: Alaska Native Language Center.

Krauss, M. 1970 (typescript). *Eyak Dictionary*. University of Alaska and MIT.

Leer, J. 1989. Directional systems in Athapaskan and Na-Dene. In: E.-D. Cook & K.D. Rice (eds) *Athapaskan Linguistics*, 575–622. Berlin/New York: Mouton de Gruyter.

Eskimo-Aleut

Badten, L., V.O. Kaneshiro, and M. Oovi. 1987. *A Dictionary of the St. Lawrence Island/Siberian Yupik Eskimo Language*. 2nd preliminary edition (with supplementary forms from revised 2008 edition). Edited by S.A. Jacobson. Fairbanks: Alaska Native Language Center.

Bergsland, Knut. 1986. Comparative Eskimo-Aleut Phonology and Lexicon. *Journal de la Société Finno-ougrienne* 80, 63–137.

Bergsland, Knut. 1994. *Aleut Dictionary*. Fairbanks: Alaska Native Language Center.

Dobrieva, E. A., E. V. Golovko, S. A. Jacobsen and M. Krauss. 2004. *Naukan Eskimo Dictionary*. Fairbanks: Alaska Native Language Center.

Fortescue, M. 1988. *Eskimo Orientation Systems*. Copenhagen: Meddeleser om Grønland, Man and Society 11.

Golovtso, E.V. 1993. *Aleutsko-russkij í russko-aleutskij učebnij slovar'*. St. Petersburg: Prosveščenie.

Jacobson, S. 1984. *Yup'ik Eskimo Dictionary*. Fairbanks: Alaska Native Language Center.

Menovshchikov, G.A. 1964. *Yazyk sirenikskix eskimosov*. Moskva/Leningrad: Nauka.

Reuse, William de. 1994. *Siberian Yupik Eskimo*. Salt Lake City: University of Utah Press.

Seiler, Wolf. 2005. *Iñupiaq Eskimo Dictionary*. NANA Regional Corporation, Kotzebue, Alaska.

Chukotko-Kamchatkan

Apalu, Artur. (No date). List of Chukchi terms for winds and directions compiled in the community of Yanrakynnot, Chukotka, for the SIKU (Sea ice knowledge and use) project 2008–9 (courtesy of Igor Krupnik).

Bogoraz, V. G. 1904–1909. *The Chukchee*. Memoir of the American Museum of Natural History, The Jesup North Pacific Expedition, Vol. 7 (ed. F. Boas), Leiden: E.J. Brill.

Bogoraz, V.G. 1937. *Luorovetlansko-russkij slovar'*. Moskva/Leningrad: Gosudarstvennoje učebno-pedagogičeskoe izdatel'stvo.

Fortescue, M. 2005. *Comparative Chukotko-Kamchatkan Dictionary*. Berlin: Mouton de Gruyter.

Golbtseva, V. (No date). List of winds at Uelen, Chukotka, compiled for the SIKU (Sea ice knowledge and use) project 2008–9 (courtesy of Igor Krupnik).

Inenlikej, P. I. 1982. *Slovar' čukotsko-russkij i russko-čukotskij*. Leningrad: Prosveščenie.

Jochelson, Waldemar. 1908. *The Koryak*. Publications of the Jesup North Pacific Expedition 6. Washington: Smithsonian Institution.

Krašeninnikov, S. 1755. *Opisanije zemli Kamčatki*. St. Petersburg: Izd. Akad. nauk.

Kurebito, Megumi (ed.). 2001. *Comparative basic vocabulary of the Chukchee-Kamchatkan language family*, 1. Endangered Languages of the Pacific Rim, A2-011. Suita: Faculty of Informatics, Osaka Gakuin University.

Radlinski, I. (compiler B. Dybowski) 1891-2. *Słowniki narzeczny ludów Kamczackich*. Kraków: Rozprawy Akademii Umiej tności, wydzial filologiczny, 16-18 (vol. 2, 3 and 4, with a further volume in 1894 on eastern Koryak – i.e. Alutor; newer edition with Russian translations 1998 as B. Dybowski, *Slovar' itel'menskogo jazyka*, ed. K. Feleško, Warszawa: Energeia).

Saryčev, G. A. 1802. *Putešestvie flota kapitana Saryčeva po severovostočnoj časti Sibiri, Ledovitomu morju i Vostočnomu okeanu*. St. Petersburg.

Volodin, A. P. and Xalojmova, K. N. 1989. *Slovar' itel'mensko-russkij i russko-itel'menskij*. Leningrad: Prosveščenie.

Xalojmova, K, M. Dürr, Æ. Kasten, and S. Longinov. 1996. *Istoriko-etnografičeskoe učebnoe posobie po itel'menskomu jazyku*. Krasnodar: Kamshat.

Zhukova, A.N., and T. Kurebito. 2004. *A basic topical dictionary of Koryak-Chukchi languages*. Research Institute for Languages and Culture of Asia and Africa, Tokyo University of Foreign Studies.

Tungusic and Yukaghir

Cincius, V.I. 1975–77. *Sravnitel'nij slovar' tunguso-man'čžurskich jazykov*. Leningrad: Nauka.

Cincius, V.I. and L.D. Rišes. 1952. *Russko-evenskij slovar'*. Moskva.

Lebedev, V.D. 1982. *Oxotskij dialect evenskogo jazyka*. Leningrad: Nauka.

Nikolaeva, Irina A.1988. Problema uralo-jukagirskix genetičeskix svjazej. Doctoral dissertation, Institut Jazykoznanija, Moskva.

Nikolaeva, Irina A. 2006. *A historical dictionary of Yukaghir*. Berlin & New York: Mouton de Gruyter.

Sem, L.I. 1976. *Očerki dialektov nanajskogo jazyka: bikinskij dialekt*. Leningrad: Nauka.

Vasilevič, G.M. 1958. *Evenkijsko-russkij slovar'*. Moskva: Gosudarstvennoe izd. inostrannyx i natsional'nyx slovarej.

Nivkh

Gruzdeva, E. 1998. *Nivkh*. München: Lincom Europa.

Gruzdeva, E. 2007. Challenging theory: spatial deixis in Nivkh. In: P. K. Austin, O. Bond & D. Nathan (eds) *Proceedings of Conference on Language Documentation and Linguistic Theory*, 103–113. London: SOAS.

Krejnovič, E.A. 1986. Ob imenax prostranstvennoj orientatsii v nivxskom jazyke. In: P. Ja. Skorik (ed.) *Paleoaziatskie jazyki*, 157–166. Leningrad: Nauka.

Mattissen, Johanna.2003. *Dependent-head synthesis in Nivkh*. Amsterdam/Philadelphia: John Benjamins.

Puxta. M.N. 2002. *Nivsko-russkij razgovornik i tematičeskij slovar'*. Endangered Languages of the Pacific Rim, A2-017. Suita: Faculty of Informatics, Osaka Gakuin University (also Russian edition: Izdatel'stvo Drofa, St. Petersburg).

Saveljeva, V. N. and Č. M. Taksami. 1965. *Russko-nivxskij slovar'*. Moskva: Sovetskaja enciklopedija.

Saveljeva, V.N., and Č. M. Taksami. 1970. *Nivxsko-russkij slovar'*. Moskva: Sovetskaja enciklopedija.

Schrenck, L. von. 1892–1900. *Forschungen im Amur Lande in der Jahren 1851-1856*, Anhang zum 3. Bind, bearb. von W. Grube. St. Petersburg: Akadamie der Wissenschaften (also for Goldi/Nanai).

Takahashi, Moritaka. 1942. *Karafuto Giriyakugo*. Osaka: Asahi Shimbunsha.

Ainu

Batchelor, J. 1938. *An Ainu-English-Japanese Dictionary.* Tokyo: Iwanami Shoten.

Hattori, Shiro. 1964. *An Ainu Dialect Dictionary*. Tokyo: Iwanami Shoten.

Kirikae, Hideo 1993. Some geographical concepts of the Ainu. In: Hiroaki Okada (ed.) *Kankyokuhokubunka no Hikakukenkyuu* (Comparative Studies in Circumpolar Cultures): 103–120. Sapporo: Faculty of Letters, Hokkaido University.

Piłsudski, B. (ed. A.F. Majewicz).1998. *The collected works of Bronislaw Piłsudski, vol. 2: Materials for the study of the Ainu language and folklore* (first publ. Cracow 1912). Berlin & New York: Mouton de Gruyter.

Radlinski, I. (compiler B. Dybowski) 1891–2. *Słowniki narzeczny ludów Kamczackich*. Kraków: Rozprawy Akademii Umiej tności, wydzial filologiczny, 16-18, vol. 1: Kurile Ainu).

Vovin, A. 1993. *A reconstruction of Proto-Ainu*. Leiden/New York: Brill.

General

Ackerman, Robert E. 1984. Prehistory of the Asian Eskimo Zone. In: D. Dumas (ed.) *Handbook of North American Indians*, vol. 5 (Arctic), 106–118 Washington: Smithsonian Institution.

Aratiunov, S.A. 1988. Even: Reindeer herders of Eastern Siberia. In: W. Fitzhugh & A. Crowell (eds) *Crossroads of Continents,* 35–38. Washington: Smithsonian Institute.

Beck, David. 2003. Tsimshianic from a Central Northwest areal perspective. In: C. Gillon, N. Sawai & R. Wojdak (eds.), *ICSNL XXXVII: The 37th International Conference on Salish and Neighbouring Languages*, 35–60. Vancouver: UBC Working Papers in Linguistics.

Black, Lydia. 1973. The Nivkh ("Gilyak") of Sakhalin and the Lower Amur. *Arctic Anthropology* X, 1–117.

Boas, F. 1909. *The Kwakiutl of Vancouver Island*. Publications of the Jesup North Pacific Expedition, vol. 5, 2.

Brown, Cecil H. 1983. Where do cardinal directions come from? *Anthropological Linguistics* 25, 2, 121–161.

Buck, Carl Darling. 1988 (original edition 1949). *A dictionary of selected synonyms in the principal Indo-European languages.* Chicago & London: University of Chicago Press.

Burenhult, Niclas, and Stephen Levinson. 2008. Language and landscape: a cross-linguistic perspective. *Language Sciences* 30, 135–150.

Carlson, R. L. 1990. Cultural antecedents. In: W. Suttles (ed.) *Handbook of North American Indians*, vol. 7 (Northwest Coast), 60–69. Washington: Smithsonian Institution.

Dikov, N.N. 1994. The paleolithic of Kamchatka and Chukotka and the problem of the peopling of America. In: W. Fitzhugh & V. Chaussonnet (eds) *Anthropology of the North Pacific Rim*, 87–95. Washington/London: Smithsonian Institution.

Dolgix, B.O. 1962. On the origin of the Nganasans – preliminary remarks. In: H. N. Michael (ed.) *Studies in Siberian Ethnogenesis*. Anthropology of the North, Translations from Russian sources no. 2, 220–299. Toronto: University of Toronto Press.

Dumond, Don E. 1977. *The Eskimos and Aleuts*. London: Thames & Hudson.

Dumond, Don E. 1987. A Re-examination of Eskimo-Aleut prehistory. *American Anthropologist* 89 (1), 32–55.

Evans, V. 2009. *How words mean*. Oxford: Oxford University Press.

Fiedel, Stuart. 1992 (second edition). *Prehistory of the Americas*. Cambridge: Cambridge University Press.

Fortescue, M. 1998. *Language relations across Bering Strait*. London & New York: Cassel Academic.

Josephy, Alvin M. Jr. 1973. *The Indian Heritage of America*. London: Penguin Books.

Krupnik, Igor. 1993. *Arctic adaptations, native whalers and reindeer herders of northern Eurasia*. Hanover & London: University Press of New England.

Lebedintsev, A. L. 1998. Maritime cultures of the north coast of the Sea of Okhotsk. *Arctic Anthropology*, 35 (1), 296–320.

Levin, M.G., and L.P. Potapov. 1956. *The Peoples of Siberia*. Chicago and London: University of Chicago Press.

Levinson, Stephen C. 2003. *Space in Language and Cognition*. Cambridge: Cambridge University Press.

MacDonald, John.1998. *The Arctic Sky*. Royal Ontario Museum and Nunavut Research Institute.

Majid, A., M. Bowerman, S. Kita, D. Haun, and S. Levinson. 2004. Can language restructure cognition? The case for space. *Trends in Cognitive Sciences*, vol. 8 no. 3, 108–114.

Mitchell, Donald. 1990. Prehistory of the coasts of Southern British Columbia and North Washington. In: W. Suttles (ed.) *Handbook of North American Indians*, vol. 7 (Northwest Coast), 340–358. Washington: Smithsonian Institution.

Nichols, Johanna. 1992. *Linguistic diversity in space and time*. Chicago / London: University of Chicago Press.

Petersen, Robert, and Lotte Rix. 1982. Klimasvingninger og grønlændernes forhistorie. *Tidsskriftet Grønland*, 82–100.

Pevnov, A. M., and A. Yu. Urmančieva. Forthcoming. Neordinarnaja izopolisemija v nekotoryx jazykax severnoj Azii.

Prokofjev, G.N. 1935. *Sel'kupskaja grammatika*. Leningrad: Izdatel'stvo institute narodov severa, Tsik SSSR.

Sapir, Edward. 1938. Glottalized continuants in Navaho, Nootka, and Kwakiutl. *Language* 14, 248–274.

Sato T., Amano T., Ono H., Ishida H., Kodera H., Matsumura H., Yoneda M., and Masuda R. 2007. Origins and genetic features of the Okhotsk people, revealed by ancient mitochondrial DNA analysis. Journal of Human Genetics 52(7), 618–627.

Scherzer, Joel. 1976. *An areal-typological study of American Indian languages north of Mexico*. Amsterdam and Oxford: North Holland.

Vasiljevskij, R.S. 1981. *Po sledam drevnix kul'tur Xokkajdo*. Novosibirsk: Nauka, sibirskoe otdelenie.

As of 2008 Museum Tusculanum Press has taken over the series *Monographs on Greenland | Meddelelser om Grønland.*

Manuscripts should be sent to:

Museum Tusculanum Press
University of Copenhagen
126 Njalsgade, DK-2300 Copenhagen S
DENMARK
info@mtp.dk | www.mtp.dk
Tel. +45 353 29109 | Fax +45 353 29113
VAT no.: 8876 8418

Guidelines for authors can be found at www.mtp.dk/MoG

Orders
Books can be purchased online at www.mtp.dk, via order@mtp.dk, through any of MTP's distributors in the US, UK, and France or via online retailers and major booksellers.
Museum Tusculanum Press bank details:
Danske Bank, 1092 Copenhagen K
BIC: DABADK KK
IBAN: DK98 3000 0005 2225 20

More information at www.mtp.dk/MoG

About the series
Monographs on Greenland | Meddelelser om Grønland (ISSN 0025 6676) has published scientific results from all fields of research on Greenland since 1878. The series numbers more than 345 volumes comprising more than 1250 titles.

In 1979 *Monographs on Greenland | Meddelelser om Grønland* was developed into a tripartite series consisting of

Bioscience (ISSN 0106 1054)
Man & Society (ISSN 0106 1062)
Geoscience (ISSN 0106 1046)

The titles in the series were renumbered in 1979 ending with volume no. 206 and continued with volume no. 1 for each subseries. In 2008 the original *Monographs on Greenland | Meddelelser om Grønland* numbering was continued in addition to the subseries numbering.

Further information about the series, including addresses of the scientific editors of the subseries, can be found at

www.mtp.dk/MoG